THE Hillier GARDENER'S GUIDES

DESIGN & PLANTING

Andrew McIndoe

A DAVID & CHARLES BOOK

David & Charles is an F+W Publications Inc. company
4700 East Galbraith Road
Cincinnati, OH 45236

First published in the UK in 2006

A catalogue record for this book is available from the British Library.
ISBN-13: 978-0-7153-2306-9
ISBN-10: 0-7153-2306-7

Printed in Singapore by KHL Printing Co Pte Ltd
for David & Charles
Brunel House Newton Abbot Devon

Produced for David & Charles by
OutHouse Publishing, Winchester, Hampshire SO22 5DS

Series Consultant Andrew McIndoe

For OutHouse Publishing:
Series Editor Sue Gordon
Art Editor Robin Whitecross
Editor Polly Boyd
Design Assistant Caroline Wollen
Proofreader Audrey Horne
Indexer June Wilkins

For David & Charles:
Commissioning Editor Mic Cady
Art Editor Sue Cleave
Production Beverley Richardson

Visit our website at www.davidandcharles.co.uk

David & Charles books are available from all good bookshops; alternatively you can contact our Orderline on 0870 9908222 or write to us at FREEPOST EX2 110, D&C Direct, Newton Abbot, TQ12 4ZZ (no stamp required UK only); US customers call 800-289-0963 and Canadian customers call 800-840-5220.

CAPTIONS
Previous page (left to right): *Allium* 'Globemaster', *Nymphaea* varieties, *Cirsium rivulare* 'Atropurpureum'
Above (left to right): *Hosta* 'Sum and Substance', *Hedera helix* 'Buttercup', *Vinca major* 'Variegata' and *Pleioblastus variegatus*, *Dryopteris erythrosora*, *Euphorbia griffithii* 'Fireglow', *Lilium henryi*

ORNAMENTAL PLANT OR PERNICIOUS WEED?

In certain circumstances ornamental garden plants can be undesirable when introduced into natural habitats, either because they compete with native flora, or because they act as hosts to fungal and insect pests. Plants that are popular in one part of the world may be considered undesirable in another.
Horticulturists have learned to be wary of the effect that cultivated plants may have on native habitats and, as a rule, any plant likely to be a problem in a particular area if it escapes from cultivation is restricted and therefore is not offered for sale.

Contents

Introduction

I am not a garden designer by profession, but I have designed a number of gardens: three of my own and 17 at the Chelsea Flower Show. In addition, I have advised many garden owners on the selection of plants for their gardens and their layouts. I like to think of myself as a gardener with an interest in and, I hope, a flair for design.

Through 30 years of involvement in the garden industry, I have been fortunate enough to be part of the most recent stage in the evolution of the English garden. Garden design as we know it evolved from landscape gardening, around the same time as a wealth of new plants was introduced in the Victorian era. But while landscape gardening was restricted to those with many acres and extensive budgets, garden design is accessible to all owners of outdoor spaces. Today it is a popular pursuit, and there is more variety in the style and content of gardens than ever before. The creation of a garden involves not only plants but also hard landscaping materials, such as timber and paving, water, furniture, pots, lighting, and an extensive portfolio of ornaments and accessories.

Not all gardeners recognize design as an important element of their garden. Like fashion, design is all-important to some and a dirty word to others. However, as a gardener you are probably already making design decisions without realizing it: where to plant the runner beans, where to position a new pot, where to plant those daffodil bulbs, where to put the compost bin. All gardeners are, inevitably, involved in design and planning, and there are basic principles that apply to all, while style is a personal thing.

Most gardens are not designed at the outset: they 'happen' over time. A little planning goes into the early stages, then evolution takes over. There is nothing wrong with this process. However, the mature garden can come closer to fulfilling the gardener's initial vision if some thought goes into the planning at an early stage.

I hope this book will give you ideas on what you can add to your garden and how the positioning of the various elements can change the picture, whether you're planning a garden from scratch or just hoping to rejuvenate the garden you already have. The main thing to remember is that garden design should not be about someone else doing it all for you. You may need help to formulate your thoughts, but your ongoing input is all-important if you want to create a personalized space that works for you.

Andrew McIndoe

INSPIRED BY CHELSEA

The Chelsea Flower Show, which started in 1913, is known throughout the world as the showcase of British gardening. New plants are launched, fashions are established, and inspiration is given to nearly 200,000 visitors who pass through the showground in less than a week. The show also attracts extensive media coverage.

Up until the 1980s, flower shows such as Chelsea were effectively the shop windows of nurseries, where plants were displayed in their prime for customers to evaluate and order for despatch or collection in the dormant season. This changed with the development of container-grown plants (which meant gardeners could buy and plant all year round) and the emergence of garden centres and retail nurseries, as well as mail-order catalogues and the Internet, so gardeners can now see what growers have to offer without leaving the house.

Many nurseries still use flower shows to sell plants, but alongside this the 'ideas and inspiration' side of gardening has evolved enormously, particularly at the Chelsea Flower Show. The show garden takes centre stage for media attention – and with it increased interest in design – and garden landscaping materials and accessories are an essential part of the overall picture. Primarily, visitors go to Chelsea to get ideas, which they can then use in their own gardens (see pages 6–7).

The Award of Garden Merit ♀

Many of the plants in this book have a ♀ symbol after their names. This denotes that they have been awarded the Royal Horticultural Society's Award of Garden Merit (AGM). To qualify for the award, a plant has to have more than one point of interest as well as a unique property. It has to be easy to grow, of sound constitution and, most importantly, a good all-round garden plant. This is not to say that a plant without an AGM is not worth growing. It means that, to date, the Royal Horticultural Society has not trialled it or the plant does not meet all these criteria.

LEFT: *Cirsium rivulare* 'Atropurpureum'.

An opulent planting of acers and rhododendrons punctuated with *Lilium regale* surrounds a brushed steel sculpture by Matt Stein. Part of 'A Writer's Garden', the Hillier exhibit at the Chelsea Flower Show 2005. Designer Andrew McIndoe.

Lessons from Chelsea

The Hillier exhibit has been the largest stand in the Great Floral Pavilion at the Chelsea Flower Show for many years. At around 400 square metres (480 square yards), it is larger than the average garden, so many of the considerations and design principles we apply when creating the show garden are relevant to anyone designing a real garden.

Building a show garden has a number of unique challenges: the plants have to be perfect for a specific week, and the garden has to be completed by a certain date, before judging and the opening of the show. More visitors come here in a few days than most gardens receive in a lifetime, and the show is ephemeral. A show garden lives on only in photographs and memories – of those who have constructed it and those who have looked carefully at it, while a real garden goes on to grow and develop. Nonetheless, there are basic design principles that remain the same.

MAKE THE MOST OF THE SPACE

Every year, visitors to the Hillier exhibit have commented on its size and scale, remarking: 'Surely it must be bigger than last year?' This means we must have succeeded in making the most of perspective and the three-dimensional aspect of the garden. The planting consists of several levels: from the trees down through the taller shrubs to the lower shrubs and herbaceous perennials. Contrasting leaf form and colour, and spreading the colour throughout the exhibit, maintain the interest of the visitor. Like an interesting narrative, a garden needs to be a combination of light and shade, loud and soft, and obvious and subtle. By dividing the area, which reveals and conceals vistas, elements of surprise are reserved for the visitor, who should see different pictures on approaching the garden from different angles.

USE FOCAL POINTS TO DRAW THE EYE

The surroundings of a show garden are unavoidable: the setting is the Pavilion – a great, purpose-built temporary exhibition hall with steel uprights, cross-braces, hanging signs and a host of other unsightly distractions. However, as the garden takes shape they 'disappear', not because they are concealed, but because there are other more interesting things to look at. When the show opens, visitors are oblivious to the unsightly features as their attention is caught by the display. As in a real garden, drawing the eye to certain focal points tends to work better than screening off an unattractive area.

BE PREPARED TO RETHINK

You can plan as carefully as you like, but the reality is often very different when you start work. We have always had to modify plans once construction has started, to take account of unforeseen obstacles. Maybe a water main is in a different position from where it was on the plan, or perhaps a pathway is 1m (40in) longer than shown. Providing you are prepared to rethink, any obstacle can be overcome, and often the finished result is more satisfactory than the original plan.

NEW PLANTS AND OLD FAVOURITES

'What are your new plant introductions this year?' is one of the most commonly asked questions in the early days of any show; gardeners and the media are always interested in anything new. However, the plants that can be guaranteed to steal the show are old favourites, such as the flowering dogwoods, Japanese maples,

Some of the old favourites that invariably steal the show: *Acer palmatum* 'Bloodgood' (1), *Heuchera* 'Amethyst Myst' (2), *Hosta sieboldiana* var. *elegans* (3), *Rosa* MARY MAGDALENE ('Ausjolly') (4), *Cornus* 'Porlock' (5), and *Rhododendron* 'Horizon Monarch' (6).

rhododendrons, azaleas, hostas, heucheras and roses. As gardeners, we should perhaps be asking 'What's good?' rather than 'What's new?'

PERSONALIZE THE GARDEN

Sometimes the smallest details are show-stealers. It is not necessarily the most expensive features that are the people's choice. Over the years, the most surprising things have captured the imagination: old tools, items of furniture, ceramic globes, coal used as pebbles, old boats, buckets and tea chests. These are the personal details that make a garden unique.

THE PLANNING PROCESS

Making a new garden, or planning to change part of an existing garden, is an exciting prospect. One of the most enjoyable aspects is gaining inspiration from books, magazines and garden visits, and shopping for plants and materials. Getting the basics right from the outset is the key to success in any design project: a little thought and planning will reap rewards later. Decisions should be influenced by the personal tastes of the garden owner but tempered by the practicalities of their implementation.

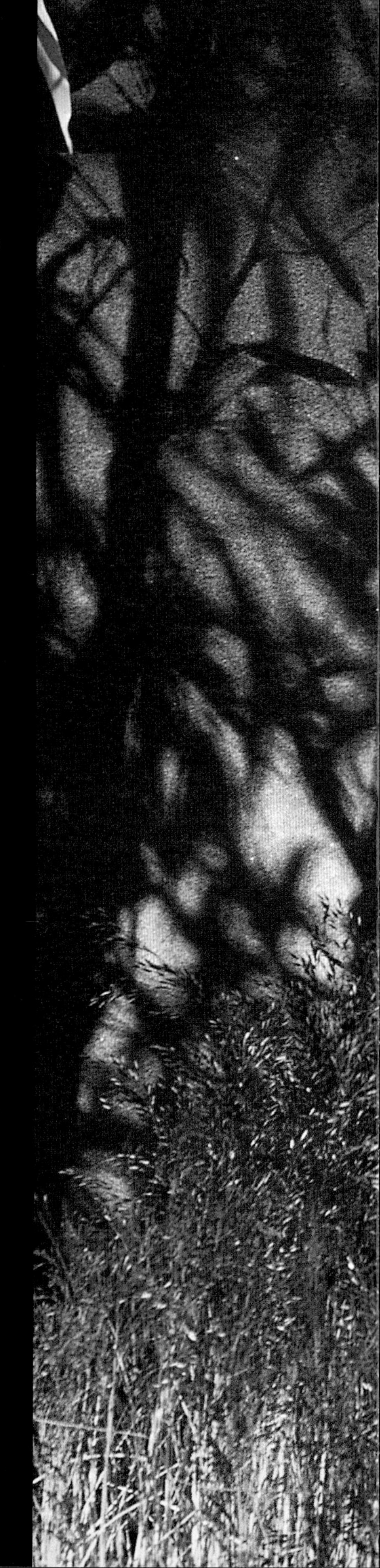

RIGHT: An elegant bamboo casts changing shadows on a rendered wall.

Consider your needs

Before you start designing a garden it is vital to take various personal considerations into account: how long you plan to live at the property, your budget, how much time you can realistically put in on a weekly basis to maintain the garden, and how you are going to use the space. Whatever you decide, the main thing to remember is that the garden needs to work for you on a practical as well as an aesthetic level.

Those on the property ladder may be looking at enjoying the garden for the next three to five years only. Where this is the case, you need to consider how the garden will appeal to prospective buyers as well as how it will suit you. An attractive, well-planned garden will certainly enhance the value of the property and make it a more saleable proposition, but while you may be keen on gardening, a prospective buyer may not, so a relatively easy-to-maintain garden will be the safest choice. If you plan to stay put, and the garden is going to be part of your living environment for the foreseeable future, you will view things differently. You can plant with the longer term in mind and can approach the development more steadily.

Whatever the timescale, it is wise not to rush into any decisions before you have lived with the garden for a time. You may be surprised to see what plants emerge once the growing season gets underway, and it enables you to see where the sun falls at different times of the year.

An attractive, well-planned garden will become a natural extension to your living environment.

YOUR INPUT

While keen gardeners are always looking for a job to do, many people take on a large garden without considering the physical effort and time involved and find it too much of a commitment. Getting the right balance between workload, energy and time is key to the enjoyment of a garden.

Plan at the outset what you are prepared to put in, in terms of time and effort. Remember, the size of garden does not necessarily relate to the effort involved. Large gardens normally require more maintenance than small gardens, but you may be able to employ a contractor to look after the grass while you tend to the borders. In a small garden, attention to detail is more important; every plant has to play its part during the year and you have to help them to work harder.

If you plan the planting carefully, you can cut down on the amount of work you

LITTLE AND OFTEN

If you can plan to spend some time in the garden every week you will keep on top of things. Split up the time and enjoy it. A few minutes' weeding after a day's work can be very therapeutic, and a little deadheading every day in summer and regular grass-cutting will keep things in trim. Weeks of neglect followed by a major onslaught at the weekend means that you may come to resent the demands on your time.

will have to do in the long term. Compact evergreen shrubs provide structure with little requirement for pruning or aftercare, and well-chosen ground-cover plants reduce the need for weeding. In small gardens it is worth considering dispensing with a lawn. Grass needs cutting every week in the summer months, so if this does not fit your time schedule then think of alternative surfaces to create open space, for example gravel, low ground-cover planting, paving or decking (see pages 48–51).

Top: This terrace has plenty of room to sit and enjoy the garden. An ornamental grid over the pond makes it safe. Above: Even in a tiny space there is usually room for a neat table and chairs.

Top: If you want to grow vegetables an open, sunny position is vital. Even a small plot can be very productive if well managed and maintained. Above: An old lawnmower planted with grasses and a subtly painted bird table help give this rural garden its traditional charm and help to create a country garden picture.

WHAT DO YOU USE THE GARDEN FOR?

Whether starting a new garden or modifying an existing one, it is important to consider what you will actually use the garden for. Looking back over the last century, domestic gardens and their uses have changed many times. They have evolved with our increased affluence and changing lifestyles. What were once production areas for vegetables and flowers have often become outdoor living areas and attractive scenes to look at from the house. Recently, some swing back towards their earlier function has seen increasing interest in productivity: vegetables, herbs and cut flowers from one's own garden have a special appeal, and the therapeutic qualities of gardening are now being recognized on a larger scale alongside the materialistic aspects of property enhancement.

A GARDEN FOR RELAXING

If you want your garden to be an 'outdoor room', or an extension to the living area of the house, you will have to plan it accordingly. New homes are often supplied with a miniscule rectangle of paving outside the patio doors, so if you want to accommodate a table and chairs for dining, you will probably have to replace the patio with a larger area of hard surface (see pages 48–51). Privacy and seclusion are important and need to be achieved without blocking light and making the area feel too enclosed (see pages 32–35.)

For families with young children, a safe play environment usually takes priority. The garden design may need to accommodate a football pitch or a paddling pool more urgently than a flower border and a potager. Although the finer planting may have to be put on hold for a few years, it does not stop the basic structure planting from being established. If you have a trampoline or climbing frame, bear in mind that an area of pine bark may be a better surface than grass, as it is awkward to move large items for mowing. Also, decking is often more child-friendly than paving, and suits modern houses. Features such as sandpits and paddling pools are easily incorporated with timber surfaces and are easily changed when these playthings are no longer required.

A GARDEN TO GARDEN IN

Established gardeners will understand the need for a garden to garden in. Those who enjoy gardening as a pastime want enough to do: cultivating, weeding, planting, deadheading and watering. All gardens require these activities up to a point, but you have to decide if the garden will fulfil your needs. A gardener moving from a large plot to a small,

Above right: In this garden with an oriental theme, a raised timber walkway is a strong visual feature but at the same time invites exploration. A design of this type would work well in a confined area because of its sense of space. The gravel with easily maintained planting would be inexpensive to install.

USE CHANGES WITH TIME

The role of the garden will tend to change over the years, according to your stage of life, so try to look ahead if the garden is a long-term proposition. For example, design the garden so that once the play area is no longer required by the children you will be able to widen the flower borders. Or once you no longer have the energy for a vegetable plot you can turn it into an area that is easier to maintain by planting shrubs and perennials with ground-cover plants.

GARDEN FASHIONS

Garden trends often follow clothing and interior fashions. As interiors have become less cluttered, so gardens have followed with simpler, cleaner designs including plenty of green foliage and fresh, soft colours. However, the experts often tell us that a fashion is over long before most of the population has realized that it has come in. Although grasses and alliums may have had their day on the catwalk, gardeners will still plant and enjoy them for years to come.

These two gardens are similar in shape; both would fit into a long, rectangular plot. The garden above is a striking, contemporary space and works well attached to a modern living environment; it changes little with the seasons and requires minimal maintenance. By contrast, the more traditional garden on the left changes throughout the year and requires input, but is probably more rewarding in the longer term.

easy-to-maintain one may be starved of enough to do, so it may be a case of adding a new greenhouse, more seasonal pots and containers, or a new mixed border to keep the interest up.

Growing fruit and vegetables is an appealing prospect for many gardeners, and is highly rewarding. Many vegetables, fruits and herbs can be incorporated into the overall design of the garden: a pot of herbs on the patio, a growing bag of tomatoes against a wall, or a wigwam of beans in the flowerbed. Before embarking on a separate vegetable plot, ask yourself whether you are able to maintain the input needed throughout the year: as with any aspect of gardening, much time and effort will be required. Also, consider when your vegetables will be ready to harvest. If you are away in the summer, the bulk of your efforts could be wasted. Also, vegetables need sun and good soil; if your garden has neither, then an area devoted to vegetables is not advisable.

STYLE AND TASTE

Our tastes are constantly influenced by fashion, the media and by those around us. However, a garden is a personal space and you are the one who has to like what you see and must enjoy living with it. Remember that tastes change with time, and what appeals to you now may not in a year or two.

When planning a garden, remember that the latest trend in garden design may look dated a few years on. Beds planted with the latest Hybrid Tea and floribunda roses, so popular in the 1960s, would be distinctly old fashioned in the 21st century. Conifers and heathers, once so in vogue, have given way to shrubs and perennials. How will we feel about tree ferns and alliums in a few years time?

As with clothing, classic style endures. If in doubt, it is better to play safe and choose something you know you will be comfortable with every day, particularly for the basic structure planting and building materials. To ring the changes in a garden, you can vary the colour of seasonal planting from year to year, use a different shade of paint or wood preservative on wooden structures, and move features such as pots, ornaments and accessories around the garden.

FINANCIAL CONSIDERATIONS

Many people budget for spending less on the garden than on the interior of the house, but this is an unreasonable expectation. Your garden will probably be larger than any of the rooms in your house, and frequently the plants and features in a garden are a longer-term investment than our interior furnishings.

How much it will cost will depend on you: the materials you choose, the size and type of plants you select, and whether you are going to do the work yourself or employ a landscape contractor. The landscaping materials used in the construction of a garden are as important as the plants themselves. Never compromise on quality – cheap paving or fencing and poor-quality turf spoil many gardens. Larger specimens naturally cost more than younger, smaller plants. If you want to give the effect of a mature garden in a relatively short space of time, but are on a budget, then invest in a few key specimen plants. These should be main structure plants and those that will be part of the landscape for the foreseeable future.

When it comes to creating a garden it is important to remember you do not need to do everything at once, but if you have some sort of plan, whether detailed or outline, you can make a start with the basic essentials and add later.

This small garden would require initial investment in terms of paving, walling and construction: most people would require professional help. Once the right planting is established it is a low-maintenance garden that will provide interest throughout the year. The selection of plants is carefully chosen to provide structure and a variety of shapes and textures, while maintaining a colour theme without the need for flowers.

Aspect and views

The direction a garden faces and the amount of sun it receives at different times of the day will have a major influence both on how you use certain areas of the garden and on your choice of plants. Surrounding views and neighbouring gardens will also have a great impact on your space.

Early morning in spring: although the sun is stronger than it was in winter, the light is filtered through the fresh new leaves of deciduous shrubs and trees.

A garden that is sunny (south-facing in the northern hemisphere) is ideal, as it gives you control and flexibility: numerous plants will thrive in sun, and you can create as much or as little shade as you like by adding trees or a structure such as a pergola (see pages 56–57). If you have a shady garden that is overshadowed by neighbouring buildings, you have to work with the shade by building it into the design and planting appropriately.

Before you do anything else, monitor the position of the sun, and the amount of light it contributes to various areas of the garden at different times of the day and year. You may think that the

LIGHT AND THE CHANGING SEASONS

The amount of light reaching a garden changes with the seasons, not only because of the position of the sun and its height in the sky, but because of the presence of the leaf canopy of deciduous trees and shrubs. The shade may be much lighter in winter once the leaves have fallen from the trees.

ADJUSTMENTS AND COMPROMISES

It is often worth incorporating elements beyond your garden into your own design – for example, a neighbouring tree or shrub could become a feature in your garden too. However, remember that the feature may not be part of the scene in the long term, and few of us have control over what happens outside our own plot – something else may block the view, and a neighbour may not cherish the plant you admire. Consider how any changes will alter your view and what steps you can take within your own garden to compensate.

Boundary fences and hedges take up space and are part of the scene in adjoining gardens. Where possible, discuss mutual requirements with your neighbours. If you can reach an acceptable compromise, it may save potential disputes later on.

A superbly positioned urn, the surrounding bright, lush planting and a fine green sward create a striking picture in this view through the dining room window.

obvious place for a patio is immediately outside the main living area of the house. However, if you want to sit in the sun, and this area does not get any during the main part of the day, then you could move the sitting area somewhere else, or have two sitting areas. Similarly, if you dislike direct sun and the area outside the house is permanently baked by it, either relocate the sitting area to a more shaded location or provide some form of shade.

CONSIDER THE VIEW

Plants in nearby gardens, surrounding trees, views over the countryside, and neighbouring walls and fences can all become part of your garden design. A garden that 'borrows' the landscape takes on a very different proportion from one that is an individual entity – while a small walled courtyard can be a self-contained picture, a similar-sized plot in a rural situation can become part of the landscape if uses surrounding views.

Garden owners often get territorial about their plots, resenting the encroachment of plants from neighbouring gardens, but before you advance with the pruning saw, consider whether the overhanging plant is actually an asset, blending your garden into part of a bigger picture. We are sometimes all too prepared to block out the surroundings with hedges, fences and screens. In a new garden, these surrounding features can make an important contribution to the early maturity.

You also need to consider the views from various rooms within the house. If your main sitting area is currently set away from the garden, and overlooks an eyesore such as a neighbouring garage, you may want to change the rooms around, or plant something more attractive in the foreground. Also, what does the house look like from the sitting area in the garden? Maybe its appearance could be improved by the addition of a climber or by taller foreground planting.

THE HOUSE AND GARDEN

The vista of a garden from the house is all-important, so design it with all of the rooms that look onto the garden, including upstairs, in mind. Consider the approach to the house if this is through the garden. If you leave the house early and return late, simple pleasures in the form of fragrant and aromatic plants can enhance the garden you pass through.

The practicalities

When planning the layout of your garden, it is vital you take into account practical considerations before thinking about the detail. You will have to consider accessibility to the garden, allow for storage space, and install electricity and water before embarking on any construction work. If the garden is on a slope or on uneven ground, you may also need to level the site or install a drainage system. Good preparation of the soil is essential before planting.

LEVELS AND DRAINAGE

Any slopes, dips and inclines of the garden site must be addressed right at the outset. If your garden slopes gently away from the house, you have little to worry about, but many plots have more severe slopes to contend with.

Lawns need to be level or on a very gentle slope. A lawn established on uneven ground will always be difficult to mow. Those gardening on sharper gradients may need to consider terracing the site. (See pages 112–115.) Lawns also need to be well drained; a simple drainage system is not difficult to install, and will prove to be very worthwhile within the lifetime of the garden.

Paved areas also need to be level, but with sufficient camber to drain effectively. Badly laid paving often harbours puddles and promotes the growth of algae in winter. On poorly drained sites, filling the gaps between the paving slabs and

Above: This pool has been successfully incorporated into a levelled area on a sloping site. Right: Timber sleepers can be used as low retaining walls on sloping ground.

Above: This raised terrace helps to solve the changing levels in a sloping garden and provides a flat space for garden furniture. The gravel joints between the paving slabs aid drainage. Right: Access to a garden needs to be considered, both for the period during its construction and for maintenance.

the area around the patio with gravel may solve this problem effectively and inexpensively. (See page 50.)

Level areas are essential for a water garden, too. Although pools will fit into sloping sites, the area occupied by water needs to be completely level or the pool will look awkward and liners and construction mechanics will be visible. (See pages 54–55.)

Where serious levelling is required, it is worth seeking professional advice; changing the surfaces on a sloping site can radically change the run-off of water after rainfall and can cause problems, particularly if the slope faces in the direction of the house.

ACCESS TO THE GARDEN

If your garden is accessible only through the house, you need to bear this in mind at the planning stage. First, there are difficulties involved in moving plants and materials through the house when constructing the garden. Later, once the garden is established, it will be difficult to take prunings, grass cuttings, compost and equipment in and out of the area.

In small gardens with limited access, low-maintenance planting is essential: slow-growing shrubs and evergreens that require little pruning and produce limited waste are the best choice. Ideally, you will also opt for a hard surface

rather than a lawn, which requires bulky equipment and somewhere to dispose of grass clippings. For owners of large gardens with limited access, it is vital to include good compost facilities. This solves the problem of disposing of garden clippings and provides all the organic matter necessary for the garden, without the need for additional soil conditioners to be brought in. A mechanical garden shredder and somewhere to store it would be an advantage.

CONSIDER STORAGE

For all homeowners, storage is a major consideration. When it comes to storing garden equipment and machinery, a shed is ideal. Make sure you choose one that is large enough to store all you need but not so large that it dominates the garden.

Top: A storage area, such as this shed, is vital in the garden. Centre left: A garden bench is easy to move, so is a good choice for a lawn. Centre right: Vegetables can be incorporated with flowers if there is no space for a dedicated area. Bottom left: Garden features, such as this wall mask, can transform an awkward corner. Bottom right: A beehive is a wildlife-friendly feature. Compost containers that are cleverly disguised to resemble beehives are readily available.

WATER AND ELECTRICITY

If you require electricity to any part of the garden, perhaps for a water feature or garden lighting, install it before you start construction. The same is true of water if you need a tap located away from the house, for example near the greenhouse or garage. If you are installing a hot tub or swimming pool below ground, it will also need to be constructed at this early stage.

THE WISH LIST

As well as planting areas, you may want to include the following in your design:

- Storage area (see above).
- Wildlife area (or even just a bird table).
- Vegetable plot (see pages 12–14).
- Play area (see pages 12–13, 21).
- Lawn (see pages 42–47).
- Sitting area (see pages 10–11, 16–17, 48–49).
- Garden feature (see pages 60–63).
- Garden structure (see pages 56–59).
- Water feature (see pages 52–55).
- Hot tub or swimming pool (see left).

DISCREET BUT ACCESSIBLE

Most people tend to locate their shed at the end of the garden, right in the main field of vision. If you position it near to the house it is less obvious and more accessible. Similarly, garden owners with young families need to consider where to position play equipment. Children's play equipment is rarely beautiful, but it is not needed for long in the life of a garden. Hiding it defeats the object: you need to be able to keep an eye on the children. Try to locate it to the side of the main field of vision and provide other interesting focal points in more prominent locations. A safe surface will be required for any play equipment.

The spreading branches of *Prunus* 'Shirotae' help to conceal this storage building. The colour-themed planting blends with the colour-washed shed, integrating it effectively into the garden.

In small gardens, storage chests are an invaluable alternative to a shed.

Frequently used items must be accessible throughout the year, so paths and all-weather surfaces are needed to connect storage areas to the house. Consider all the items you will need to store, remembering compost containers, waste bins and water butts. If the garden has a lawn, the storage place for the mower needs to be in close proximity and ideally on the same level.

Bicycles need to be easy to access and get in and out of the garden, and barbecues also need to be accessible in summer. Gas barbecues, which can be kept on the patio all season, or even all year round, are the best choice. For drying clothes, a rotary clothes drier is best as it is compact and can be removed when not in use. It needs to be positioned over dry ground and requires considerable space around it when opened out.

EXISTING SOIL

The quality of your garden soil depends on the history of the plot. An existing garden that has been well cultivated

MECHANICAL HELP

In larger gardens, mechanical help is invaluable. A garden tractor is worth considering, being useful for cutting the grass and for pulling a trailer. This carries a far larger capacity than a wheelbarrow and can be used to transport materials and collect garden waste. A mechanical shredder is useful to shred prunings for composting. This avoids trips to the recycling centre and generates useful compost for soil improvement.

Whatever equipment you need, it is worth consulting a specialist dealer and investing in machines that are robust enough to do the job. Cheap garden machinery can be a false economy.

will present few problems. However, new gardens may be more challenging, particularly those of newly built properties. (See pages 148–53.)

The type of soil and its condition should play a key part in your selection of plants. For this reason, it is extremely important to know the pH of the soil – this is the measure of acidity or alkalinity: soils with a low pH are acid, while those with a high pH are alkaline. A pH check is always worthwhile: use either a soil pH check kit (see box, below) or a pH meter. The latter is easier to use and is a good way of checking all parts of the garden. The ideal is to have a neutral to slightly acid soil, as this will support the widest range of plants successfully. Some plants will grow only on certain types of soils: rhododendrons, azaleas, camellias and other ericaceous plants need an acid soil and will not grow on those with a high pH. Plants in neighbouring gardens are a useful clue to the soil type and what will grow successfully in the area.

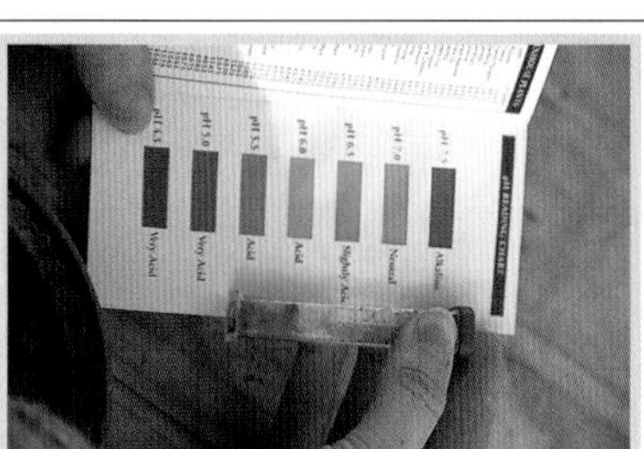

SOIL TESTING

Soil pH can be assessed using a soil test kit (above) or a pH meter, and is measured on a scale of 1–14. The closer the pH to neutral (pH 7) the wider the range of plants you can grow; acid soil has a pH value below 7; alkaline soil has a pH value above 7.

IMPROVING THE SOIL

In areas with poor-quality soil, sound preparation and soil improvement before planting will reap rewards. It is possible to modify most soil types by adding soil improvers and fertilizers. However, it is always much better to choose appropriate plants that suit the soil type rather than trying to fundamentally change the soil to suit the plants.

A deep, well-drained, fertile soil that does not dry out provides the ideal growing conditions, but in reality few gardens are blessed with it. However, you can improve the structure of most soils, making water and nutrients more available to the plants. Light, sandy, stony

Above: Ericaceous plants, such as this beautiful *Rhododendron* 'The Hon. Jean Marie de Montague', thrive on acid soil and should be avoided by those gardening on alkaline soil, that is with a pH greater than 7. Left: Before undertaking any planting, fork over the ground thoroughly and remove all weeds.

FEEDING THE GARDEN

Most soils carry an adequate supply of plant nutrients for growth, but for the best possible results supplement this with a slow-release general fertilizer with trace elements. The three main plant nutrients are Nitrogen (N), which is used for the growth of shoots and leaves, Phosphorus (P), which is used for root growth and establishment, and Potassium (K), which is used in flower and fruit production. The ratio of each of these major nutrients to one another is usually shown on the fertilizer pack and is shown as N:P:K. Consider what plants you are growing and what you want them for and choose your fertilizer accordingly. Roses, for example, need a fertilizer that is high in potash for blooms and nitrogen for healthy foliage. A newly planted shrub will benefit from plenty of phosphorus for rapid root establishment. A fertilizer with 7:7:7 on the pack contains equal parts of each nutrient. Trace elements are smaller quantities of nutrients required for healthy growth, good leaf colour and other plant qualities and functions.

In the intensely cultivated environment of a garden, supplementary feeding is necessary for some plants. Roses benefit from annual feeding with a proprietary fertilizer.

and chalk soils are improved by adding copious amounts of organic matter; it increases their water-holding capacity and gives them more body. Heavy, clay soils are improved by the addition of organic matter and fine gravel or coarse grit, as these create a more open structure and make the soil easier to work.

Before planting, dig over the soil and remove all weeds. Any perennial weed with a persistent root has the ability to regenerate from the tiniest fragments left in the soil, so a systemic, non-persistent herbicide is the best solution, applied when the weeds are in full growth. This may need repeating in heavily infested areas. Annual weeds often appear in great numbers in the first year. Digging turns up new seeds that may have been dormant for a season or two. These can be dealt with in the same way, although gentle hoeing will remove them as effectively if done regularly when the seedlings are small.

A general slow-release fertilizer provides all the nutrients necessary and is usually the best choice when planting new plants or feeding established ones. Sprinkle the granules around the plant and fork the soil lightly around the base.

A mechanical cultivator is useful to turn over soil that has been well cultivated in the past. On compacted ground, deeper cultivation is required: deep digging to twice the depth of a spade or fork to break up the subsoil is the best solution.

The principles of design

The aim of garden design is to create a pleasing picture – an inviting landscape that you want to live with – but it is not always easy to know how to achieve this to best effect. Certainly, taste, style and your personal requirements come into the design decisions you make to a large extent, but there are also certain tried-and-tested principles of garden design that are likely to help you during the early stages of the planning process.

The Float Garden, Chelsea Flower Show 2005. Show gardens are inspiring but you must decide whether this style of garden suits your property.

The first issue to consider is the location of your garden and the style of your house. It is vital that the garden suits the property to which it is attached. An image in a glossy magazine or a display garden at the Chelsea Flower Show may be what you aspire to, or may fire the imagination, but ask yourself what that style of garden would look like attached to your property. Is the mood right? Is the scale right? Are the plants and materials used in keeping with the building materials of the house? Generally, highly contemporary designs rarely sit well alongside rural properties, and traditional country gardens can look out of place in a modern setting.

PROPORTION AND SCALE

Whatever size of garden you are working with, and whether it is a new plot or an existing garden you are remodelling, you should be aware of the proportion of planting and features to open space. The basic rule is one-third planting to two-thirds space. Without the space, the planting and features within the garden cannot be seen to best advantage.

GET IDEAS

Books, magazines, television and garden shows are all an excellent source of inspiration. So are other people's gardens. Take a look at properties similar to yours. What has worked? What mistakes have they made? Once you start to identify the factors that make a garden work you are well on the way to creating or improving your own.

In a small garden, this amount of space may seem daunting; however, it can consist of many different elements – lawn, paving, gravel, water, decking and pebbles. In a tiny garden, such as an enclosed courtyard, some of that space can be vertical: plain walls, perhaps optically enlarged by the presence of mirrors or trompe l'oeil. Features such as summerhouses, gazebos, arches and pergolas can be considered part of the planting space.

When it comes to beds and borders, space really matters. In most gardens, borders are too narrow and the beds are too small. All gardeners underestimate how large plants grow, and often how quickly. A 60cm (2ft) wide border along a fence line is hardly adequate to accommodate a climber and a few diminutive perennials, let alone a small shrub or two. The minimum width for a border should be 1m (40in), and that will restrict what can be grown to dwarf shrubs and modest perennials. It is preferable to have a border 2m (6ft) wide, and 3m (10ft) is better yet. If you intend to incorporate three layers of planting in a bed, then you need an area of at least 3 square metres (3 square yards).

In successful garden designs there is the right balance between space and planting. In this scheme, a large part of that space consists of water.

Planting areas need to be sufficiently large and wide to be effective. This bed of herbaceous perennials takes up considerable space when the plants are in full growth and flower in summer.

A pleasing picture is created when there is interest at all levels. In this garden, at le Clos du Coudray, Normandy, the design includes all the qualities of a beautiful natural landscape, from the height of the trees to the depth of the water.

PLANTING LAYERS

To create a pleasing picture, try to introduce a variety of heights, both in planting and in features which will act as focal points. Below eye level are the hard surfaces and the pool or pond if you have one. This layer also includes the detail planting: low ground cover, most annual bedding plants, bulbs, dwarf shrubs and low herbaceous perennials. Eye level is the main field of vision – one that you will look at directly from the windows of the house. It is a colourful and interesting part of the picture. Plants in this layer include the majority of shrubs, herbaceous perennials, taller bulbs such as lilies, roses and shorter climbers. Also at this level are garden features such as statues, ornaments, furniture, fences and gates. Above eye level you have the part of the garden that makes it three-dimensional. Trees are the most important plants here, influencing light and shade. Tall shrubs stray into this area, as do the tallest herbaceous perennials. Climbers also fill this space, not only on walls and fences, but in a more dominant way on arches and pergolas, providing essential vertical interest. This planting level is much in evidence when viewing the garden from the upstairs of the house.

Most gardens lack interest in one of these levels, usually above eye level. This results in flat, uninteresting gardens

LEVELS IN THE NATURAL LANDSCAPE

The three levels of planting and interest are present in the most pleasing natural landscapes, and create an environment we feel comfortable in. A predominantly green country scene with trees, hedges and fields is friendly and unthreatening. A more barren landscape without vertical interest may be inspiring but it rarely feels inviting or somewhere you want to spend much time on a regular basis.

that are missing vertical interest. We are often afraid of plants getting too large, especially trees. Usually, this is the result of poor selection and the wrong advice. There is a tree or tall shrub for every space – it is just a matter of selecting the right one. (See pages 72–75.)

AN ILLUSION OF SPACE

A garden can be made to appear larger or smaller according to where plants and objects are located and their relative positions. There is a tendency to put large plants and objects towards the back of the garden or border and smaller ones at the front, but this is not always the most satisfactory solution. Height in the foreground, providing it does not block the line of vision, increases perspective and makes the garden appear longer.

Light, see-through plants are often good in the foreground. (See page 105.) Similarly, a structure such as an arch or pergola in the foreground with a view to a focal point beyond creates a longer vista than the same view without the foreground interest. (See page 56.)

THE GARDEN PICTURE FROM ABOVE

When planning the garden, always consider the picture from an upstairs window in the house – the first floor tends to give the clearest view. Shapes of garden areas and how they relate to one another are not always evident when you are in their midst, whereas from above they become much clearer. It is also easier to see the proportion of planting in relation to the rest of the garden from upstairs: as a rule of thumb, gardens are ideally composed of one-third planting and two-thirds space. A few large, well-designed planting areas look a lot better than numerous small ones.

Focal points are essential in all successful designs. They concentrate the attention and draw the eye to particular locations within the picture. Specimen plants, colourful flowers and foliage, gates, containers, ornaments and buildings can all act as focal points. Carefully positioned focal points lead the eye and have a profound effect on perspective and the illusion of space in a garden.

The use of height in the foreground and light, airy plants rising above the rest of the planting add depth to a planting scheme.

AN ELEMENT OF SURPRISE

A good garden design does not reveal all of its features at first glance. The garden visitor should be encouraged to explore and discover further treats and rewards. In tiny gardens, this is possible if you carefully position plants and features. In a larger garden, it may be best to divide the area into several 'rooms', one leading on from the other, yet with each room independent of the next. This works particularly well in long, narrow gardens. (See pages 142–43.)

Shapes of planting areas

Designing the shapes of lawns, borders, patios, paths and flowerbeds can be difficult without the plan appearing contrived. As a rule, the simpler the layout, the more successful it is likely to be. Generally, curves suggest informality and tend to suit country gardens, while geometric designs suggest formality and are often more fitting for urban situations.

Above: Curved, informal beds follow the lines of the slope. Right: In this small formal garden the straight lines of the border follow the boundaries but the design succeeds because of the plentiful planting and bold central feature.

There are, of course, exceptions to the rules. For example, the traditional cottage garden was often formal in layout, with a straight path leading to the front door and dividing the plot into two rectangles flanked by wide borders. But the layout became soft and informal in appearance with the addition of random and prolific planting.

In most cases, the lines of the design should not run parallel with the boundaries of the garden: in so many

THE IMPACT OF PLANTING

Planting has a major impact on a garden's design, often breaking up the distinct lines and shapes of the framework. Some of the most successful garden design partnerships have combined geometric formality with informal planting. The architect Edwin Lutyens and designer and plantswoman Gertrude Jekyll worked together on many schemes in the early 20th century, incorporating geometric ground design softened by bold, opulent planting. In a similar way, the formal framework of the garden at Sissinghurst Castle, Kent, designed by Harold Nicolson, was softened by the wild informality of Vita Sackville-West's passionate planting. Both partnerships divided large areas into smaller garden rooms appropriate to formal design.

A straight brick path leads through deep planting areas, the shape of which is hidden in the billowing growth of a richly planted midsummer border.

modern gardens a plain rectangle of grass is flanked by narrow, fence-hugging borders that only draw attention to the boundaries. However, in a small enclosed space, such as a walled courtyard, where the boundary is a feature and part of the garden structure, this design works well.

Avoid contrived curves that are unnecessary to the design. The wavy-edged border along the edge of the lawn is an easy trap to fall into, but it will look awkward and unnatural on the ground, even if it pleases the designer on paper.

FEASIBILITY

When planning your garden, spare a thought for feasibility: consider how you will construct it and whether it is possible to create the shapes you visualize with the materials you have in mind. There are often simple ways to overcome construction problems. For example, rectangular paviors can be used in a curved space without the need for cutting if gravel, stone chippings or low plants are used to fill the irregular spaces between them and the line of the curve.

Privacy and concealment

In most gardens there is a need to enclose space, around the periphery of the garden or around certain areas within it. This may be to define the boundaries, to provide security, to break larger areas into smaller 'rooms' or to block out undesirable views within or beyond the garden. How this privacy, concealment and division are achieved has a profound effect on the garden's appearance.

Above: In a large garden there is room to use hedges to enclose and divide the space and provide both privacy and a means of hiding the less attractive features of the garden. Right: A trellis top on a traditional fence is ideal for climbers such as honeysuckle (*Lonicera*) to grow through.

Before you put up a fence or plant a fast-growing screen to provide privacy and security, consider the implications: enclosure may reduce light and air circulation; it may make the garden feel claustrophobic and could block views of attractive aspects of adjoining gardens. Instead, a few strategically placed plants may be all the screening that is necessary for privacy, and a light barrier can often provide sufficient security.

FENCES

The utility fence panel is usually rather unattractive and in the early life of a new garden will be very visible. Cheap fencing can be improved by planting a hedge in front of it – perhaps ***Carpinus betulus***, ***Fagus sylvatica*** or ***Thuja plicata***. However, a better option may be a more attractive, good-quality fence that can be further enhanced with a few climbers.

Solid fences are visible barriers. Often a heavy trellis or palisade screen affords similar privacy without making the garden feel so enclosed. A compromise is to use a low, solid fence with a heavy trellis top, which gives height without the weight. A trellis top can be added to existing fencing (as long as it is sound), to increase the height and the privacy it offers without the need for total replacement.

Wire fences offer little privacy and look institutional and utilitarian. However, they are effective at keeping animals in or out of the garden and can be transformed by using them as supports for trained shrubs such as **pyracantha**, **ivy** (*Hedera*) or **cotoneaster**. When clothed in vegetation they become attractive, as well as effective, living screens. (See also page 142.)

WALLS

Walls are an expensive option because of the high cost of building them, so few people nowadays create a completely walled garden from scratch. In most gardens, any walls there are tend to be low and used for short boundaries, retaining walls and raised beds.

A low wall, about 1m (40in) high, makes a superb base for a palisade or trellis screen. This is further enhanced if brick or block columns are incorporated between the timber panels. In settings that are contemporary or Mediterranean in feel, or in a coastal garden, concrete building blocks, which are rendered and then colour washed, can be an effective and inexpensive alternative. They combine well with bleached, natural or colour-washed timber.

Foundations are required for any wall, and this can be a good way to lose unwanted brick and concrete rubble. A concrete foundation is not as daunting to construct as it sounds, but should be in depth equivalent to at least one-quarter of the height of the wall.

Top: Trellis panels on this wall break up the expanse of brick and provide support for climbers and wall shrubs. Above left: Classic iron railings set on an ivy-covered wall do not steal light or space from the garden. Above right: Stone-coloured render transforms a concrete block wall into an elegant backdrop.

HEDGES

In larger gardens, dividing the area is often desirable from both a design point of view and a practical one. Hedges and screens are used to create individual garden rooms and to hide less attractive areas of the garden (see page 32).

Bear in mind that hedges take up space in a garden. A young container-grown hedging plant may look slim and innocent when planted, but by the time it develops middle-age spread it may be occupying much of the garden. A hedge can also take water, light and nutrients at the expense of other plants. Similar privacy may be achieved with informal planting of structural evergreens that contribute more to the garden picture and do not require regular clipping (see pages 76–79). When dividing areas with hedges, plan the width of the hedges at the outset, or the spaces between them may in time become impractically small.

NEAT HEDGES

Where the neatness and formality of a clipped hedge is required, choose an appropriate plant for the size of hedge needed and clip regularly from an early age. Do not leave clipping until the plants have grown beyond the height and spread required, as clipping back at this stage will result in a woody, bony hedge. If clipping starts at an early age, dense, well-branched plants result. (For hedging plants, see pages 76–79.)

TREES

Often the main objective in providing a screen in the garden is to prevent the house and garden from being overlooked by neighbouring houses. Perhaps a neighbour has extended their property or a new house has been built where previously there was an open view. A large evergreen or conifer may seem like the obvious solution, but these have the disadvantage of width and weight at the bottom of the plant, when the problem area is in fact above eye level. A better solution may well be a deciduous tree. Although it loses its leaves in winter, the framework of the branches is still there and, as well as being attractive, this will provide a light but effective screen. Some trees come into leaf earlier or retain their foliage longer than others, for example ***Pyrus calleryana* 'Chanticleer'**♀ (see page 146) and ***Crataegus laevigata* 'Paul's Scarlet'**♀ (see page 73). A tree provides a moving, changing picture to look at, as opposed to the solid barrier of a functional, fast-growing conifer.

Top left: Used to divide a garden, a beech hedge is an interesting feature that changes with the seasons. It is especially lovely in winter when the low sun filters through the copper leaves. Below left: An evergreen barrier of *Euonymus fortunei* 'Emerald 'n' Gold' on rustic post-and-rail fencing.

FOCAL POINTS

Drawing the eye to focal points elsewhere often works better than screening an unattractive object or area. By providing something interesting to attract the attention, the offending view becomes insignificant. The focal point could be a statue, a pot, a specimen plant or a garden structure; it does not need to hide the eyesore and is usually best placed in the foreground. The eye then focuses on the attractive object while the ugly one disappears into the distance.

HIDING THE HORRORS

There are certain necessary evils in any garden that can become unsightly focal points if not cleverly disguised. If you plan how you are going to screen or conceal them at the outset, they can be incorporated into the layout and therefore made less conspicuous.

Where a water butt is in a prominent position, a traditional wooden barrel may be worth the investment. Similarly, a well-made timber compost container tends to look less conspicuous than a plastic alternative, especially when it is surrounded by appropriate planting in the vegetable garden.

Manhole covers are a problem and invariably occur in the most inconvenient places: in the middle of the patio or in the centre of the lawn. You can replace the cover with a pre-made grid, which you can buy from a builders' merchant, and fill it with pebbles, cobbles or even carpet planting. This can be extended to the area around the grid to integrate the cover into the surroundings. Another idea is to use the position to site a feature such as a pot or birdbath. The cover then becomes a focal point rather than an eyesore and is still readily accessible.

NATURAL MATERIALS

Plastic compost bins and water butts can be made more attractive by wrapping them with willow or reed screening. This is inexpensive and easy to install, and blends more easily into planting than the shiny plastic material these objects are often made from.

Above: A strategically placed tree fern, *Dicksonia antarctica*, is an exotic feature that both screens and draws attention away from the shed behind. Right: A trellis panel draped in *Hedera colchica* 'Sulphur Heart' and *Lonicera similis* var. *delavayi* makes an effective screen for an oil tank.

Air-conditioning units are best screened by well-positioned planting – far enough away to allow the air to circulate. An evergreen shrub, such as ***Elaeagnus* × *ebbingei*** or ***Prunus lusitanica***♀, will usually do the job effectively. In the case of high-level units, a compact-headed tree or ***Photinia* × *fraseri* 'Red Robin'**♀ (see page 79) grown as a standard is more controllable than a vigorous climber grown against the wall of the house. This will need careful maintenance to prevent the plant from interfering with the unit.

Sheds and utility buildings are more often than not positioned in the wrong place in the garden. People tend to put them at the far end of the garden. However, this is often the most visible area from the house, meaning the shed is the main focal point. If located close to the house, not only will it be more accessible but it will be far less visible and easier to integrate into the design.

Refuse bins also need to be located near the house. Self-adhesive covers are available for plastic bins with the objective of making them more attractive. In fact, they often make them more obvious and are best avoided. Instead, a folding wooden screen is often the best solution or an evergreen shrub that responds well to trimming, such as ***Viburnum tinus*** (see Good Companions, pages 79, 133) or ***Lonicera nitida***. If space will not allow for the width of a shrub, use heavy trellis clad with a large-leaved **ivy** (*Hedera*).

Drawing up a plan

Once you have formulated your ideas for your garden, it is worth taking the time to produce a simple scale plan of the design, using squared paper and a pencil. Where you go from here will depend on whether you intend to go it alone or seek professional help.

Getting your ideas down on paper will help you to visualize the proportion of open space to planting. Drawing the plan on squared paper makes it easy to measure the distance between buildings, features and plants that you want to incorporate: you will quickly see whether your ideas fit into the space you have available.

Some professional but practical garden landscapers will be happy to work from your sketches. A professionally drawn-up plan and specification is a more secure blueprint. Choose whichever option suits you better, but remember that the living part of the garden can never be entirely controlled: that is its magic.

THE EXISTING PLOT

The first stage is to draw a plan of the existing plot. Use graph or squared paper and choose a scale that allows the plan to be as large as possible on the paper you are using; 1cm = 1 metre (1:100) is ideal. Plotting the site is of course easier if it is perfectly rectangular. It rarely is. You will need a long and durable tape measure. Plot the outline of the house and the farthest corners of the plot first, checking measurements from one fixed point to another.

Next, mark any existing features that will stay in position: this may include trees and shrubs you are going to keep, existing buildings and any obstacles, such as manhole covers. It is also worth plotting any major features in the area surrounding your plot, such as a large tree in a neighbour's garden: not only for its visible effect on the design but also for its effect on light reaching your garden.

Mark the direction of the sun, where it falls at certain times of day, and any permanent shadows.

TAKE PICTURES

The photo survey is a valuable tool in redesigning an existing garden. By laying tracing paper over the pictures, or by drawing on digital prints, you will be able to see the likely impact of decisions you are planning to take. Always bear in mind what is around a plant that you are considering removing, and what is beyond it. Take pictures throughout the year to remind you of the high points and low points in the garden's year, and to evaluate the impact of sun and shade in different seasons and at different times of the day.

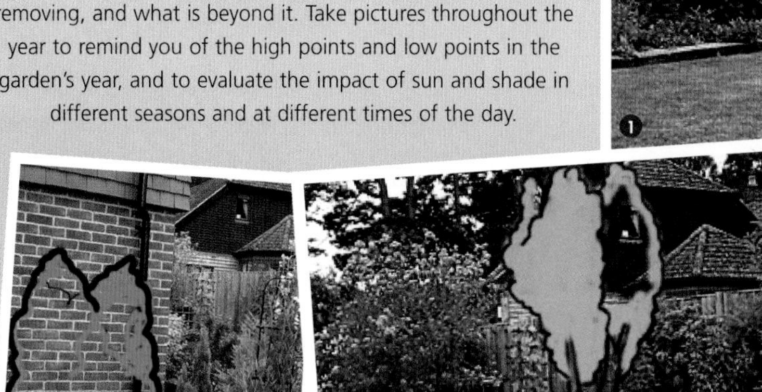

Sketching ideas onto digital prints: (1) A border with large shrubs would hide this fence and link the garden with the mature trees beyond. (2) A large evergreen would hide the water butt. (3) A strategically positioned tree would screen the house and block the view from its windows into your garden. (4) Evergreen shrubs would hide the dustbins and soften the stark brick walls. Something with scented flowers would be a good choice.

THE NEW LAYOUT

Once you are satisfied with your plan of the existing site, start to introduce your ideas into the design. It is a good idea to use sheets of tracing paper laid over the original plan so that you can experiment with various options. As you introduce elements of the design, keep visualizing what they will look like from the principal viewpoints: the windows of the house (don't forget the upstairs windows), the main seating area(s), the point of entry, and looking back towards the house.

It is important not to make your layout over-complicated. Clean lines and simple shapes will always work best: less is often more when it comes to design. Remember that the plants will provide the detail, and will soften the harder lines of the ground plan.

SEEING THE PLAN IN 3D

The next stage is to picture what your initial sketch plan will look like if it becomes a three-dimensional garden. Would a tree or tall shrub there screen the windows of a neighbouring house? Would the summerhouse look better at the end of the garden or to one side? Should there be a pergola over the terrace?

The easiest way to evaluate these ideas, particularly changes you might make to an existing garden, is by means of a simple photographic survey. It doesn't matter whether you are a good photographer or not; take pictures of the garden from all the angles from which you will view it. Take plenty, and do not get creative; photograph it just as it is. You will be surprised what you see in a photograph but did not see in real life.

Digital photographs are ideal; print several copies, on ordinary paper, of each of the most useful angles and draw in the options, using a soft-leaded pencil or felt-tip pen. Alternatively, lay tracing paper over a photograph and sketch on to that. This exercise will really make you think about how everything fits together in the garden picture.

This is a useful way of evaluating the scale of the plants and features you plan. Many people find scale difficult to judge. Go out and measure the height of several existing features and mark the measurements on the prints. Then use these to judge the height of things you are thinking of incorporating. For example, a fence panel may be just under 2m (6ft) high, while a tree you plan to plant may be 5m (16ft) high in five years' time: estimate one against the other.

Adapting an existing garden

There comes a time in any garden when some redesigning becomes necessary. No garden stands still – some plants will get too large for their position, and either the garden will have to change to accommodate them or they will have to go. Or perhaps you have purchased a property with an established garden and would like to make some minor changes to it.

When you are considering buying a property with an established garden, it is worth looking closely at the plot, as well as the house. The aspect is important, but that is not the only factor you should consider. Although you can tell a lot from what is growing in the garden and the health of the plants, some problems can be hard to see, particularly in winter. Keep an eye out for weed infestations, especially on clay soils, and in rural areas look out for deer and rabbit damage: you may need to invest in fencing. Perhaps mature trees and woody shrubs need attention. Make sure you know what you are letting yourself in for.

If you build a conservatory you need an attractive view to look at. This may mean redesigning the garden.

This difficult patch of grass and the angular retaining wall were transformed into an elegant terrace edged by a rill. Plentiful planting in the surrounding ground and in containers on the paving softens the stone and joins the garden with the house.

BUYING A GARDEN

'A mature, well-stocked garden' – this is a phrase often seen in estate agents' details, but what does it mean? Will the garden be planted to your taste? It may look good when you see it for the first time, but will there be colour and interest all year round? The only way you will know will be to live with it for a year and see what comes up: hopefully any surprises will be pleasant ones.

LIVING WITH THE GARDEN

You may feel that the garden you have inherited is not planted to your taste, but if you live with a garden for a time it often changes the way you feel about it and the plants growing there. Something that does not appeal initially may become a plant or feature you appreciate once you understand how it fits into the picture. Sometimes a plant can be made much more acceptable by adding others that work well with it. For example, a large yellow conifer may look too prominent and out of place in the garden, but if it is combined with bold, gold-variegated shrubs, such as ***Elaeagnus* × *ebbingei* 'Limelight'** and ***Euonymus fortunei* 'Emerald 'n' Gold'**♕ (see page 81), it can become a more integrated part of the planting. Add some plain evergreens, such as ***Choisya ternata***♕ (see page 38), and the prominence of the yellow will be diluted. Similarly, unattractive hard landscaping can be softened and improved by the right planting.

If you have inherited a garden shed that is unsightly and positioned in the wrong place, it can often be made more acceptable if draped in a pretty rambler, for example ***Rosa* 'Goldfinch'**. A wash of

PRUNING A FORSYTHIA

(1) A mature shrub immediately after flowering. (2) Remove some of the oldest branches right at the base of the shrub. (3) Cut back to just above where new shoots are emerging. (4) Pull out the cut branches carefully. (5) The framework is more open, allowing space for new growth, which will flower next season.

Mature yew hedges can be cut back to the bare wood to rejuvenate them and reduce their size.

Choisya ternata

Ribes sanguineum

subtle colour over the wood can change its significance in the garden and help it fit better into the design. It can also be made to appear much smaller by planting a spreading tree to stand over it.

MAKING CHANGES

It is always much harder to make changes in a garden that you originally created; after all, it was your work in the first place. You know how much effort you put into looking after the plants and how rewarding they have been over the years.

Often the most difficult decisions are those involving mature plants that are past their peak. Old deciduous and evergreen shrubs are structural features in the garden and they may remain unattractive for some time if hard-pruned. Some will come back quickly if treated harshly; others will sulk. To reduce the size and impact of the task, carry out the changes gradually rather than undertake a massive cull in one go.

OVERGROWN SHRUBS

Evergreens that make good hedging plants usually respond well to hard rejuvenation pruning. ***Viburnum tinus***, ***Elaeagnus × ebbingei***, ***Prunus lusitanica***♀ and ***Prunus laurocerasus***♀ (see pages 77–79) all take harsh treatment and can recover to make fine specimens.

Choisya ternata♀ can be very slow to recover if cut back hard; in the case of a broad shrub, remove whole branches to reduce its size, then lightly prune the remaining branches. Most **ceanothus** and **cistus** resent pruning and it often proves fatal. As both grow quickly and flower impressively from an early age, removal and replacement is the answer.

REJUVENATING LILACS

Mature lilacs can reach 5m (15ft) in height. In Victorian shrubberies, they were cut down every year to 90cm (3ft) across all the branches: this treatment results in straight, upright stems with flowers across the top of the shrub, an ideal shape for the back of a border. Grown in this way they are a more realistic choice of shrub to grow to provide structure behind other shrubs, roses and perennials, particularly when draped with a climber for summer interest.

Most conifers cannot be hard-pruned to rejuvenate them or reduce their size. A large specimen of ***Chamaecyparis lawsoniana*** that has been beheaded to reduce its height is an unattractive feature in any garden, and removal is the only solution. Unusually for a conifer, **yew** (*Taxus baccata*, see also pages 76–77) responds well to hard-pruning. Mature yew hedges can be cut right back to the bare stems to reduce their width. Do one side at a time.

Old specimens of early-flowering deciduous shrubs, such as **forsythia**, **flowering currant** (*Ribes*) and **lilac** (*Syringa*) can be rejuvenated by cutting out some of the most mature branches down to 60cm (2ft) or even lower. If you do this immediately after flowering, new vigorous shoots will develop.

Plants that grow too large for the situation and will be ruined by pruning are the most difficult to decide on. ***Magnolia* × *soulangeana*** is one of the most common examples. A beautiful broad, large shrub with a wonderful branch framework, it produces unattractive, straight, vigorous growth when pruned. The only solution is to selectively remove entire branches back to the ground or to the main stem. It may also be possible to remove the lower branches and raise the canopy, to allow planting beneath.

Magnolia × soulangeana – a large shrub that does not like pruning. Think before planting one.

PLANNING AHEAD

If you do not need to remove an existing mature shrub immediately, you may be able to plan its replacement. Perhaps there is room in the border to plant something to take its place in a year or two. A pittosporum, ceanothus (above, *Ceanothus* 'Concha') or rhamnus would grow quickly, and could be ready to take over when it has been removed. If you cannot plant a replacement in advance, it may be worth investing in a mature specimen (see page 152).

REMOVING BIG SHRUBS

Large, established shrubs are not easy to remove. Do not make the mistake of cutting the plant down to ground level before trying to dig it out. Instead, remove the branches but leave at least 1m (40in) of the stems above ground. Dig around the plant to expose the roots, removing a broad trench on all sides, and where possible, cut through any roots 60cm (2ft) or so from the stems with a sharp spade. You should then be able to use the remaining stems as a lever to loosen and eventually remove the plant.

If you want to plant in the same spot, it is important to dig out as much of the root as possible. In the case of trees and large woody shrubs, such as laurels, it may be necessary to employ a contractor with a grinder to remove the stump. If the plant was healthy, the chippings can be used as mulch or composted.

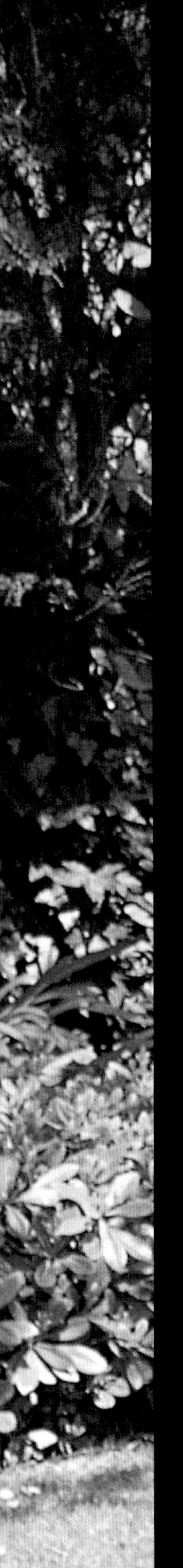

APART FROM THE PLANTING

In most gardens only one-third of the space will be occupied by planting. Two-thirds will consist of open space and permanent structures. Hard surfaces, lawn and perhaps water occupy most of the horizontal open space, while garden buildings, pergolas, arches and gazebos provide height and solid impact. Features such as birdbaths, sundials and statues become focal points in the garden picture. All these elements together create the set for the plants – the real stars of the garden stage.

RIGHT: A blue seat makes a bold focal point in a shady corner of Denmans, Sussex.

Lawns

A lawn occupies a large amount of the open space in most gardens. As a dominant feature, its shape and design in relation to the rest of the garden are of paramount importance in creating a pleasing picture. How the grass is cut, its condition and its colour, all have a radical effect on a garden's appearance. If you want to transform a dishevelled garden, the most effective thing you can do is to mow the lawn: it will improve the overall look instantly.

A well-cut lawn that is in good condition has a profound effect on the appearance of any garden, large or small.

In a square or oblong plot, a round or oval lawn will have a totally different effect from that of a square or rectangular area of grass. The round or oval lawn will result in borders of varied width, softening the corners with deeper planting. The square or rectangular lawn will have a more formal appearance and may make the space appear larger but starker.

TIPS FOR A BETTER LAWN

- If you normally cut the grass very short, set the mower slightly higher. The grass will appear a better colour and will stay green longer.
- Grass goes dormant in dry weather; it does not die. It will recover quickly once the soil is moist enough, so save water for the flower border and vegetable garden. Once the grass has started to grow again, apply a soluble lawn fertilizer to stimulate growth.
- Buy a good-quality lawn rake with spring steel tines. Rake out patches of moss regularly, as they appear, to prevent infestation.
- Treat lawn weeds regularly with a weedkiller specially formulated for lawns. Ideally, apply the weedkiller using a pressure sprayer, which can be directed onto the weeds only, rather than indiscriminately across the whole lawn.

This immaculately cut rectangular lawn echoes the shape of the garden. It makes the garden appear larger and creates a formal feel.

Mowing around this large pot is possible because of the brick-edged paving. The impact of a bold focal point in a grassed area is maintained.

Whatever shape of lawn you choose, consider the practicalities. A lawn needs mowing and maintenance; it must be easily accessible with machinery. Tight corners and narrow grass paths between beds are a problem that will be encountered weekly in the growing season. When establishing a new lawn it is worth considering how you will cut it at the outset. Turf will need cutting just a couple of weeks after it is laid, seed after around six weeks.

Tiny lawns are a problem to maintain. However small the area, a mower is needed and this requires storage. Manoeuvring a lawnmower in a small space is awkward and frustrating and limits the surrounding planting. It may be better to consider alternatives to create an open space, such as paving, gravel, thyme and sedum, and low ground-cover shrubs.

MOWING THE LAWN

Choosing the right mower is vital to the final appearance of the lawn. During the growing season, a mower will be used weekly; its reliability is paramount. Do not buy the cheapest mower, or the smallest; it will be false economy.

A well-cut lawn with stripes can be achieved with a rotary or cylinder mower. Rotary mowers are generally easier to handle, more robust and a better choice for the average lawn. Cylinder mowers give a wonderful finish on perfectly level, fine lawns. One drawback of this kind of mower is that the grass box is normally at the front, which means planting will have to be sufficiently far back from the edge of the lawn to allow for this.

On average to large lawns, always choose a self-propelled mower; it can be very hard work pushing a mower when the grass has been allowed to grow longer than usual. On sloping land, a machine with a full grass box is heavy when mowing uphill.

Some mowers mulch the grass by depositing the finely chopped cuttings back on the lawn. This avoids having to dispose of them but does not give the best results on fine lawns. Even mulch mowers that direct the clippings down to the grass roots leave a deposit that will be picked up by those walking or playing on the grass. On larger areas, make sure you choose a mower with a big enough grass box; the necessity to empty it many times when mowing becomes laborious.

Serious lawn owners should consult a garden machinery specialist before investing in a lawn mower.

MOWING UP TO THE EDGES

Whatever the shape and style of your lawn, you must be able to mow up to the edge of the beds, as this avoids unnecessary use of shears. Overhanging plants may look attractive but will be an obstacle; this is one reason why the width of borders is so important (see page 25). Consider how you will be able to turn the mower at the end of the lawn. If this is impossible without stepping onto the borders, then you will need to rethink the design.

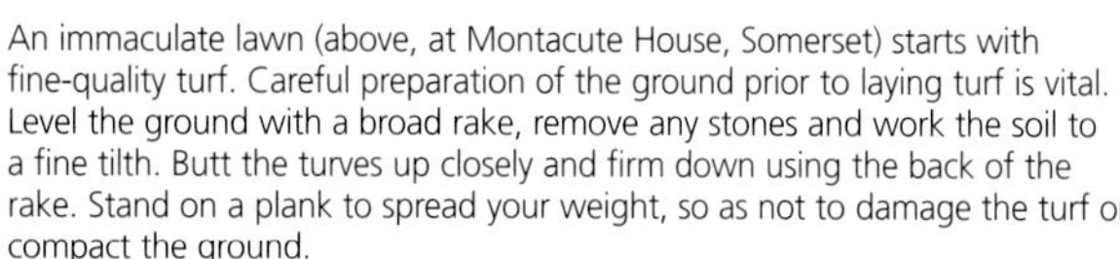

An immaculate lawn (above, at Montacute House, Somerset) starts with fine-quality turf. Careful preparation of the ground prior to laying turf is vital. Level the ground with a broad rake, remove any stones and work the soil to a fine tilth. Butt the turves up closely and firm down using the back of the rake. Stand on a plank to spread your weight, so as not to damage the turf or compact the ground.

STARTING FROM SCRATCH

A lawn is a plantation, consisting of thousands of individual grass plants. In other areas of the garden, the needs of individual plants are considered and accommodated, and competition with other plants is taken into account. Similar principles should be employed when you are trying to establish a lawn. Thorough ground preparation is essential, and good cultivation will reap rewards. Don't hurry the preparation stage – saving time at the beginning will cost hours later.

Good drainage is vital for a healthy lawn. On heavy clay, incorporate sharp grit and well-rotted organic manure, or recycled green household waste. On light soils, just add the organic matter. Cultivate, leave and re-cultivate. Eradicate perennial weeds by applying a non-residual systemic weedkiller when weeds are in active growth; let them die and resprout, if they are going to, and apply again. Remove all stones by picking them out by hand; these will come to the surface and damage the blades of the lawn mower if not removed. On a poorly drained site, land drains are the only solution. If in doubt, take professional advice.

Whether you choose seed or turf, levelling of the ground is essential. Dips and bumps do not disappear when the grass has grown, and they are obstacles when mowing. An uneven lawn will result in scalped areas and patches of long grass, which are difficult to put right later, so get it right at the outset. After preparation, leave the ground to settle to ensure there are no soft spots that will develop into depressions. Apply a general fertilizer about two weeks before the lawn is sown or turf is laid.

SEED OR TURF?

Whether you choose to sow seed or lay turf, never compromise on quality and buy the right product for the job. It is surprising how much is spent on other aspects of the garden, furniture for example, but how little on the lawn. The best times to lay turf or sow grass seed are in mid-spring and early autumn.

Seed is cheaper than turf, and there is a wide choice of grass seed mixtures to suit any situation. Great advances have been made in grass breeding, largely because of the demand for grass mixes that will withstand sports activity. Fortunately, many of these highly advanced grasses are available for the domestic lawn. Grass seed will be more evenly sown on a large area if a spreader is used. Sow lightly once up and down the lawn, and once across at right angles to the first application. Adopt this principle when applying lawn fertilizer later. Never sow seed too thickly; heavy sowing will result in competition between grass plants.

Turf gives quick results but is far more expensive than seed. As turf is arduous to lay on large areas, you may want to employ a contractor recommended by a reputable turf supplier.

Germinating grass seed and newly laid turf require plenty of water, so avoid making a new lawn in hot, dry periods. If allowed to dry out, turf shrinks and gaps result that will need to be filled with soil – a tedious job best avoided by watering well. Avoid walking on newly germinated grass and newly laid turf as this causes damage and delays establishment.

ADDING GRASS WITHOUT A LAWN

In small contemporary gardens, where limited space makes grass impractical, a token lawn can be grown in a container. A modern round bowl, cubic pot or rectangular trough can look very effective when carpeted with turf. Regularly clipped with shears, it adds essential emerald green to the garden – and the smell of freshly cut grass. Placed near a seating area, a container lawn is a tactile surface and adds life while maintaining a feel of open space. A container lawn can be started from turf or seed grown on loam-based potting compost.

A newly seeded lawn should appear thin to start with to allow space for the grass plants to grow and develop.

BUYING LAWN SEED AND TURF

Always buy turf from a specialist turf grower, not from a supplier who cuts a field and lifts the turf. When selecting seed, decide what you will use the lawn for. If the lawn is mainly to look at and will only be walked upon, choose a mix of fine tufted grasses; the grass will be of fine texture and a bright green colour. If the lawn needs to cope with heavy foot traffic and children's play, choose a mix containing dwarf perennial ryegrasses that grow horizontally and are more hardwearing. If wear is likely to be average, choose a good-quality, general-purpose mixture of tufted and creeping grasses.

The best way to improve the condition of any lawn, particularly in a garden on poor, well-drained soil, is to apply a good-quality lawn dressing.

REJUVENATING A LAWN

A lawn is a stressful environment for grass plants: growing close together, they compete for air, light, nutrients and water. Over the years, foot traffic and mowing machinery compact the ground and cause wear and tear. Damp conditions encourage the growth of moss, which competes with the grass. If neglected, the moss builds up and may take over. Just killing the moss is not the answer; the dead material will still be there around the base of the grass plants. Even without moss, dead grass leaves and stems build up, forcing the new grass growth further and further up the plant. This dead material is known as thatch.

A neglected fine lawn can usually be saved and regenerated. With aeration, scarification, feeding, moss and weed control the grass can be improved immensely. If coarse grasses have already taken over and a fine sward is required, then removal of the existing lawn and replacement with good-quality seed or turf is the only solution.

The appearance of a neglected lawn has to get worse before it improves. However, within three months, poor turf can be turned into a respectable sward. Avoid the temptation to use quick-fix solutions; these are short term, and if the objective is to create a better lawn in the long term, the source of any problem has to be tackled.

AERATING THE SOIL

Aeration increases the amount of air reaching the grass roots and improves drainage. The easiest way to do this is to

plunge the tines of a digging fork into the turf to a depth of at least 15cm (6in) every 30cm (12in). Hollow-tine aerators do an excellent job and are particularly useful on badly drained sites. These remove a core of soil using sharp, tubular tines; they do not compact the sides of the hole and so do a better job. This should be done in late winter or early spring.

On a larger area it is better to use machinery; various mechanical aerators are available for hire or to buy.

MOSS CONTROL

Moss control can be carried out in autumn or early spring. Once the moss killer (usually based on iron sulphate) has been

applied the moss quickly turns black. You can then remove dead moss with a spring-tine lawn rake, a powered lawn rake with wire tines, or with a scarifier. It is usually best to kill the moss before raking or scarifying, to prevent it from spreading. However, if infestations are severe, it is better to rake first, then apply the moss killer to allow it to penetrate.

SCARIFICATION

Scarification is best achieved with a powered scarifier. This has hook-like tines that remove the thatch and moss down to soil level. The hooked construction of the tines pulls out the thatch and creeping grass rhizomes, allowing more space for the choicer tufted grasses. This thinning process promotes better air circulation through the lawn and allows rainfall to penetrate. The scarification process should be carried out in early spring; it can be done after moss control and will then remove the dead moss at the same time.

APPLYING A LAWN DRESSING

This is the most beneficial treatment for any kind of lawn. A quality lawn dressing based on sifted loam, sand and a soil conditioner will rejuvenate the soil immediately beneath the grass and will penetrate where the ground has been aerated. It will make the ground more receptive to feeding and prepare it for oversowing if necessary. It is particularly beneficial on poor, sandy soils and thin chalk soils.

FEEDING THE LAWN

The key times to feed are autumn and spring. Autumn feeding builds the grass over the winter, resulting in a strong, dark green sward in spring. Spring feeding is carried out after aeration, scarification and the application of a lawn dressing. In both cases, a granular formulation applied using a spreader is the best choice. Solid fertilizers take longer to work, releasing the nutrients gradually. The more expensive controlled-release fertilizers give the best results, feeding the grass evenly and avoiding scorched patches caused by irregular application.

WHICH FERTILIZER TO CHOOSE?

There are many types of lawn fertilizer to choose from: those that just feed, and those with a combined mosskiller and/or weedkiller. In dealing with a neglected lawn it is better to deal with one problem at a time rather than using a combined treatment. Combined fertilizers are ideal for healthy lawns with light infestations of moss and a few weeds.

DEALING WITH WEEDS

Lawn weeds are best dealt with in late spring or early summer, after you have fed the lawn. This is because fertilizer and lawn dressing will get the weeds growing vigorously along with the grass, making them more susceptible to treatment. Use a proprietary lawn weedkiller, and apply it using a watering can or a sprayer.

SOWING EXTRA SEED

After you have removed the moss, scarified the lawn, and have applied lawn dressing, it may be worth oversowing the lawn with some extra seed. If there are bare patches and thin areas, then a light application of a good-quality seed mixture will help to thicken the lawn, improving its appearance. Take care not to sow too much – no more thickly than shown in the photograph above.

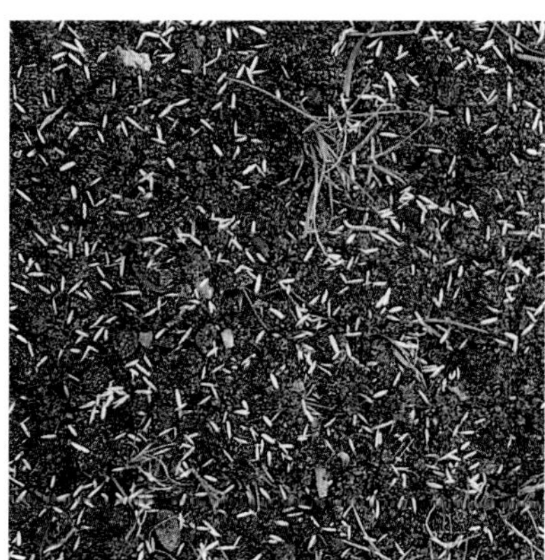

Hard surfaces

In most cases, a considerable proportion of open space in the garden consists of hard landscaping, a term that refers to hard surfaces underfoot, walling, fencing and buildings or other structures. The planting is the soft landscaping. It is often difficult to decide on the hard surfaces, such as paving and decking, as these are long-term installations that require effort and financial investment. It is important to choose materials that suit both the property and the garden.

Irregular pieces of slate and pebbles are combined successfully to create this path with steps. The geraniums soften the paving, their pink blooms echoing the colour of the pebbles.

Where a hard surface is inherited, decisions need to be made before progressing with the rest of the design: utilitarian, unattractive paving slabs do not improve with time. It is better to replace them at the outset, even if this means delaying progress with other aspects of the garden. With the vast range of natural stone and aggregate products available, there is always a better alternative – one that will transform the garden in the long term.

Before committing to any materials, take some samples home and try them in your garden; it is the only way to be certain that you are making the right choice. Have a look at the colour and texture against the building materials of your house. Look at them through the windows of the house at various times of day, wet and dry, and imagine a much larger area of the material. Will it fit the style of garden you are planning to create? Will it stand the test of time?

PAVING

Paving is the usual choice for sitting areas in English gardens: a solid, level surface is the best choice to accommodate garden furniture. Manufactured paving slabs vary from very basic to highly sophisticated

An interesting combination of bricks, flints and turf: careful trimming of the grass will be needed to maintain the effect.

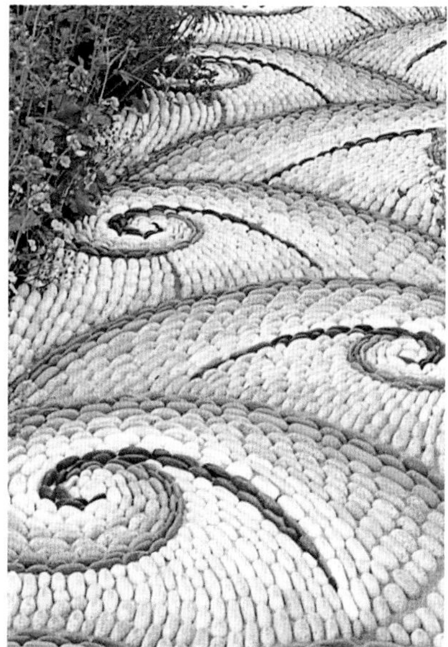

Patterns made with pebbles of different colours set in mortar make an individual feature (top left). Fill awkward corners with gravel or pebbles to avoid cutting paviors (top right). Random slabs in gravel create an informal path (above). Sets and small paviors are ideal for curved areas (above).

CHOOSING PAVIORS

Smaller paviors are lighter to handle and easier to lay; larger slabs are more difficult but cover more ground. As a rule, smaller paving units suit smaller spaces and larger ones are a better choice for large areas of paving. Mixing the size of slabs makes the surface more interesting and breaks up large expanses; it has a more informal feel.

Mixing colours rarely works and looks contrived and garish, whereas mixing materials can work if it is well done: for example, bricks with paving slabs or flints or pebbles with natural stone. Gravel combines well with solid paviors; it softens the area and is a good way of avoiding cutting slabs to fit.

If a paved area is used as a main thoroughfare at all times of the year and in all weathers, safety is an important consideration. Smooth slabs become slippery when wet, particularly in shaded areas where algal growth is a problem. A non-slip surface, and one that can be easily cleaned with a stiff broom and pressure washer, is the best choice.

TAKE CARE WITH GROUTING

Grouting involves filling the gaps between the paviors with a mixture of sand and cement. This takes skill, and paving is often spoilt by careless grouting. Use a dry mixture with little water: cement will stain the paving if it adheres to it. Press the grout firmly into the gaps using a small trowel; if it is not done properly, gaps will result when the mortar dries. Use plenty of sand in the mixture and choose the colour of sand to suit the paving: some building sand is very orange, making a strong-coloured mortar mix that can look unsightly between the paviors.

imitations of natural stone. Imported natural stone compares favourably in price with the imitation product.

Good-quality manufactured paving slabs normally offer greater consistency, especially if all requirements are purchased at the same time. Production batches can vary in colour with the raw materials used, so if this is a concern never buy a few at a time. Natural stone, on the other hand, offers subtle variations in colour and texture, which are part of its charm. The manufactured product is normally easier to lay than natural stone; the latter can vary in thickness and it is therefore harder to achieve a level surface.

Any paved area is only as good as its foundation. A solid base of hardcore and some type of compacted base material is essential. The slabs are then laid on a mix of sand and cement. Slabs laid on sand will move in time, caused by the passage of water between them. Laying paving needs a certain amount of skill and is hard work: if in doubt, seek professional help; it will be well worth the investment.

Drainage is important with paving. Some paviors, particularly those with irregular edges, look better with wider joints between them. These can be filled with gravel rather than mortar; this will aid drainage and avoid puddles.

STONE CHIPPINGS AND GRAVEL

Gravel and stone chippings are inexpensive and provide an easy way of creating a hard surface in the garden. The stone pieces in gravel are more rounded and usually make a softer, looser surface than chippings, which tend to bind together to create a firmer surface. Both can be refreshed by adding another layer of material and by raking. Plants love to encroach on gravel or chippings, softening the edges. They are not a good choice for the tidy-minded, especially the smaller-grade stones, which tend to scatter, but

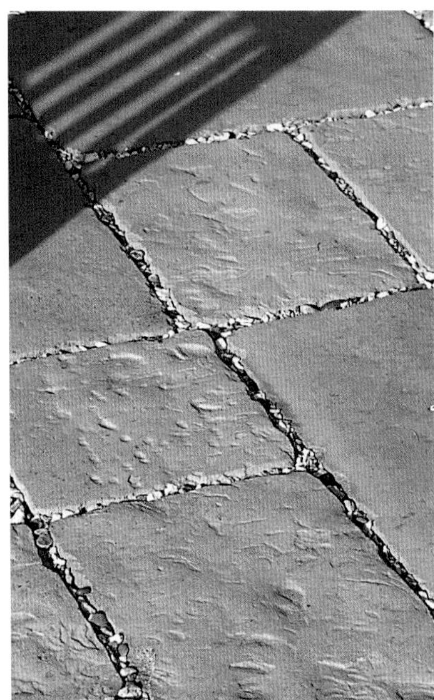

Traditional York stone is the ultimate hard surface (top left). The gaps between manufactured slabs can be filled with gravel (top right) to soften the effect. Stone chippings, slate scree or gravel (above) offer easily installed alternatives to paving. The addition of planting enhances the informal look.

CHOICE OF GRAVEL AND STONE CHIPPINGS

Choose soft colours that are sympathetic with plants and the building materials of the house, as well as any other hard landscaping materials in the garden. Large grades of stone chippings scatter less and are not as easily picked up on the shoes of those walking over the area. Angular stone chippings bind together more efficiently and do not move as much as the rounded stones of small-grade gravels.

they are a good choice for paths, and the sound made by movement on gravel conveys a feeling of security if used on approaches to the house. They make a relatively non-slip surface, so are safer than other hard surfaces.

Gravel and stone chippings can be laid directly onto compacted earth if you want plants to seed into it; this will include weeds of course. Alternatively, a firmer surface is achieved by laying on a more solid base such as that used for paving (see opposite). A weed-control membrane can be used under the gravel to prevent plant and weed growth. If you use a membrane, it is a good idea to put it under a layer of aggregate material such as scalpings. These are angular pieces of stone combined with smaller particles of sticky clay that bind together when laid and rolled over the membrane, making a firm surface and preventing excess movement.

DECKING

Decking suits contemporary designs and coastal gardens and, of course, any property where timber features as a main building material. In country gardens, simple heavy decking associates well with water but rarely looks at home attached directly to an older property.

Decking is often perceived as cheaper than stone alternatives: this is not necessarily so. It needs the same solid base as stone paving, as poor foundations lead to problems. Concrete or level existing paving is an ideal base, so it is a good choice to lay on top of an old area. Unlike paving laid on top of existing paving, it will not cause new drainage problems.

In wetter climates and in shaded areas, decking can be slippery in winter. Bear this in mind when installing it and use ridged boards or cover them with wire mesh. Decking requires a reasonable level of skill to install. For those not competent in basic carpentry, professional help is the answer.

Wooden decking suits contemporary designs and works successfully alongside water (top) and in combination with pebbles or gravel (above).

CHOICE OF DECKING

Wooden decking boards are laid out to take the full force of the weather: rain, sun, snow, frost and wind. High-quality, heavy boards, pressure-treated with the right preservatives, are essential. Cheaper, thinner boards will quickly warp and twist becoming dangerous and unsightly. Whatever the quality of decking, the time and effort taken to install it is the same, so never compromise on the quality of the materials.

Water

Water adds another dimension to the garden. The mirrored surface of still water introduces reflections, increasing the height and depth of the landscape, while moving water brings life and sound. Water also provides another habitat within the garden, where the activity of fish and wildlife can be enjoyed, and where aquatic plants and those that thrive in wet conditions can be cultivated. Any garden, however tiny, can accommodate a water feature of some kind.

An old boat makes a romantic focal point at the edge of this informal pond.

A formal pool softened by lilies and irises in the water and see-through planting in beds around it.

A pool should be appropriate to the style of garden, and its size needs to be in proportion to the space surrounding it. This may seem an obvious statement, but installing a pond is hard work, and requires soil excavation and removal. Mark out the lines of the proposed pool using a hosepipe or pegs and lines and, to give a more realistic impression, cover this area with polythene and live with it for a few days to make sure the shape and size is right.

Any open water, however small or shallow, is a potential hazard to children and animals. If this hazard cannot be overcome, a water feature such as a pebble pool is the answer (see page 63). For informal pools where wildlife could stray into the water, consider a shallow beach margin.

The situation of a pool is important to its success as a habitat. An open situation is best, away from overhanging trees that will cast shade and deposit leaves into the pool. If water lilies and flowering marginals are to be grown successfully, they need sunlight. If the garden is on more than one level, thought needs to be given as to where the pond is located in terms of height: since water runs downhill, a naturalistic pond should logically be at the lowest level in the garden. If it is at a higher level, the design of the garden needs to convey a reason for it.

If streams and cascades are to look natural, they need to start from somewhere and lead to somewhere. This is not difficult to achieve if the associated hard landscaping and planting is planned at the outset.

FORMAL AND INFORMAL POOLS

The design of a pool should follow the lines of the garden. Informal pools suit gardens with curved lines and relaxed planting. Formal pools suit formal gardens, but can also be used in square and rectangular paved areas when they follow the lines of the house. Circular pools fit in both formal and informal situations.

Areas of informal water work best when attached to and associated with surrounding planting. Marooned in the middle of the lawn, they look out of place and without reason. The scale of the surrounding planting needs to be in proportion to the area of water: large pools need bold background planting, and plenty of it. The large informal pool and a mound of soil decorated with a few small rocks and even smaller plants tends not to work well.

WATER PLANTS

Some of of the most beautiful herbaceous perennials grow in water or in wet soil. Those grown in the pond should be planted in fabric planting containers. These are much better than plastic baskets: they sit firmly on the shelves of the pool and the edges can be turned down to the required height. Once the surface of the soil in the containers is covered with washed gravel, they quickly blend into the picture. Always use proper aquatic soil to plant water plants; ordinary container composts are not suitable.

For clear water and a healthy pool, a balanced ecosystem needs to be achieved. This means introducing a mixture of marginal plants and submerged aquatics. Plants with floating leaves, such as water lilies, cut down the amount of light reaching the water, thereby slowing algal growth; this is what makes the water go green. Submerged oxygenating plants are essential for the animal life in the water.

Water adds great depth to the landscape in the Keukenhof gardens, Holland (top). Moving water is carried above the planting in a series of timber channels in this contemporary scheme (above).

Above: Plentiful planting has successfully concealed the edges of this pond. Below: A pond should be deep enough to accommodate lilies and fish, and shelves should be made at different depths for a variety of other aquatic and marginal plants. The edges of the liner can be concealed with edging stones or under a shallow pebble beach, which looks most natural if the stones are of different sizes.

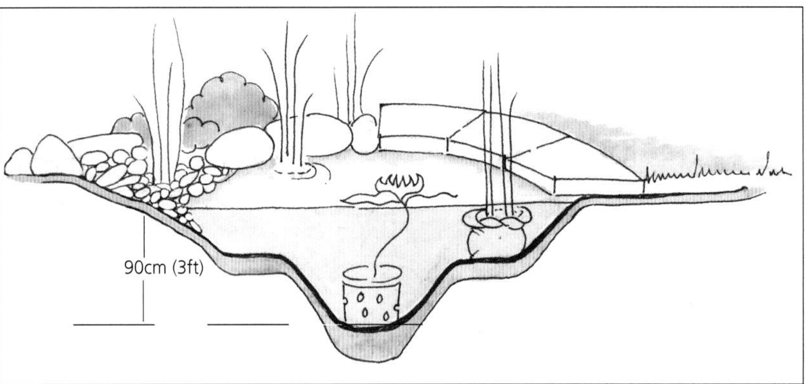

CREATING A BARREL POND

Where space is limited, or safety is a concern, a barrel pond is a delightful way to introduce open water with little effort. A good-quality half-barrel, livestock water trough or synthetic bowl can house an assortment of plants, including miniature water lilies. Once mature, it will attract wildlife and can become a successful habitat. Wooden ramps help frogs and toads to gain access, and the top of a planted container dressed with gravel and submerged just under the surface will act as a shallow beach.

Not only are marginals such as reeds, rushes and water irises an important part of the pond environment, their strong vertical lines add light height and movement as well as deep reflections.

CREATING A POND

Small ponds can be excavated by hand, but larger ones may need the help of a mechanical digger. It is surprising how much soil comes out of the hole; plan where this is to go before you start.

For a pool to support fish and water lilies, it should ideally be 90cm (3ft) at the deepest point, as this will allow 60cm (2ft) of water over the top of any planting containers in the bottom of the pool. Shelves are needed to accommodate other aquatic and marginal plants requiring shallower water.

It is crucial that all the pool edges are level before the liner is put in place, or it will be visible where the margins are higher, once the pond is filled with water. This looks unsightly and the liner can be damaged if it is exposed to sunlight.

Decide how to deal with the edges at the outset; this is imperative if the liner is to be successfully hidden. If the pool is to have a stone edging, allow sufficient overhang to conceal the liner. The stone or paving used must be wide enough to be safely secured. If the pool is edged by grass, pebbles or planting, the liner needs to run under the ground 15cm (6in) or more below the surface. This is achieved by creating another shelf around the outside of the pool, and by bringing the liner to the surface of the ground 30cm (12in) or so away from the edge of the pool. When this shelf is filled with soil or pebbles, it creates a wet margin, which can be used for planting or to create a beach. These will make the pool appear more natural.

The sides of the pool should slope slightly between each of the various levels of the pool to avoid collapse during

LINERS AND UNDERLAY

Always use a good-quality liner made from butyl rubber or the equivalent, guaranteed for over 20 years. Cheap liners are false economy, as they lack flexibility and can leak. To calculate the size of liner needed, the retailer will need to know the maximum width, length and depth of the pond.

A tough fabric underlay is available for use under butyl liners. This is excellent protection for the liner and well worth the investment. The fabric can be laid in one piece or cut to fit. The main thing is that all sides and levels are covered. It is worth using any off-cuts to add a second layer on the bottom and on the shelves.

BENEFITS OF A RILL

A rill is an effective, low-maintenance way of introducing water into an area where space is limited. It adds variety to a flat surface, whether paving or lawn, and creates a wonderful perspective, especially if there is some movement of water along the rill. This is easily achieved with a pump at one end creating a gentle current. Rills fit into traditional and contemporary gardens and create a feeling of seclusion when incorporated around a terrace.

construction. Avoid tight angles in small pools; these result in awkward creases in the liner that are difficult to conceal. All levels need to be excavated 10cm (4in) deeper than the final depth required, to allow for a generous layer of sand underneath the liner.

Remove all stones from the sides and bottom of the hole: a sharp object can puncture a liner once it is pressed against it by the weight of the water. On stony soils, add 15cm (6in) of sand at the base, and 10cm (4in) on the shelves; cover as much of the sides as possible with sand, softening the angles between the sides and each level. It is a good idea, particularly on stony soil, to cover the sand with underlay as extra protection against stones that may work their way up through the soil (see box, above).

Look out for any objects near the pool that could cause damage to the butyl liner, then lay the liner loosely over the hole. Start to fill the pool: the weight of the water will slowly drag the liner into the hole and mould it to the shape. It is necessary to guide the liner all the way, encouraging neat folds where you want them to be. Once the pool is completely full, it is worth leaving it for a day or so to settle before dealing with the edges.

The edge of the pool makes or breaks the effect; take care to finish this well, or the pool can look unsightly around the edges. Beware of the folds of the liner at the edges, particularly in the corners of the pool. Press these down tightly, or water may drain from the pool, causing a sudden drop in levels.

This rill brings life to the edge of a raised area of paving. Bordered on one side by timber sleepers, the excavated trench is lined with fabric underlay before the butyl liner is fitted. The liner needs to be plenty long enough, to allow for folds as it turns the corner. The water in the rill is deep enough to support less vigorous water lilies (left) and marginal plants.

Garden structures

A garden building can be more than just a storage shed; it can be an important garden feature and a major focal point in the design of the garden. Similarly, an arch or pergola goes beyond its function as a support for a climber and offers both interest and a third dimension to the garden. Some structures, such as summerhouses, gazebos or arbours, provide a place to sit and enjoy the garden scene from a different perspective.

This interesting pergola is well positioned to create perspective. Pergolas and arches encourage exploration of what lies beyond them, particularly when the eye is led to a well-positioned focal point.

Most gardens are flat, so anything that contributes height is a bonus. A pergola or arch is an excellent way of achieving a known quantity of height and structure, and the effect is immediate. Plants take time to grow and add maturity to a new garden; even a newly planted tree will take a year or two before it starts to fulfil its role and fill the overhead space. For instant height, a wooden structure is an excellent alternative. Climbers grow quickly, so a pergola clothed in a fast-growing subject, such as a wisteria, quickly makes an impact.

A pergola may be used over a pathway as a walk-through feature, or it could be positioned over a terrace to provide shade and create an air of intimacy and enclosure. An arch is nearly always a walk-through feature, and by nature creates an entrance to the space beyond.

Pergolas and arches are available ready-made and partially assembled. When you choose one, make sure that it is substantial enough in structure and appearance. Often the uprights are lightweight and make insufficient impact when installed in the garden. Make sure an arch is wide enough; do not forget that the width will be reduced when the structure is clothed in climbing plants.

When positioning a pergola, consider the planting at the same time. A pergola will create an area of shade, ideal for growing shade-loving plants. When a well-planted pergola is draped in climbers a leafy oasis is created beneath it, either alongside the path, if there is one, or at the base of each post. This creates a balanced picture and makes the pergola look like an integral part of the garden rather than an awkward structure that has just appeared without reason.

The same is true of an arch. If the arch rises from a base of structural planting it looks as if it belongs there; if it rises from bare earth or low planting, it may look awkward and top heavy.

POSITIONING AN ARCH OR A PERGOLA

The most important thing to remember when positioning an arch or a pergola is that there has to be a reason for it. A structure of this type draws attention and leads you on to explore: to what? Nothing looks worse than an archway positioned over a path that leads nowhere. A feature at the end – a gate, a stone urn or a large pot – and associated planting could complete the picture and make sense of the arch.

Above: a classic pergola with solid brick uprights and heavy timber rafters; the planting alongside and beneath it anchors the structure in the garden. Right: a metal frame clothed in ivy creates a living arbour.

SOLID PERGOLAS

Large pergolas benefit from substantial uprights and rafters. Gertrude Jekyll used brick-built uprights and heavy oak rafters balanced by a brick path and bold planting on and beneath the structure. This formula takes some beating. Lightweight timber uprights can be made to appear more substantial by cladding opposite sides with timber boards a few centimetres wider than the posts. If the whole structure is then stained in a dark wood colour, it appears more solid.

GARDEN ARBOURS

A garden arbour – a structure that houses a seat – is an easy-to-position feature with a purpose, perfect for a small garden or area of a garden. It can be made into an attractive space with associated planting, and its very presence implies a mood of relaxation. Consider what you will be looking at when you are sitting in it. Will you be enjoying a view of the garden or a view of the house? Positioning an arbour on one side of the garden looking towards a feature on the other side may be the most pleasing solution.

Ready-made arbours are widely available and, like garden furniture, come in various qualities and designs. Choose one that suits the style of garden but

A traditional summerhouse is successfully integrated into the garden by plentiful planting.

also one that is usable. The seat needs to be substantial and comfortable (usually cushions are essential). Those with a built-in storage box underneath are useful for storage of cushions and other items during the summer months.

SUMMERHOUSES

The summerhouse is generally intended to be a pleasant retreat in which to sit in the shade and admire the garden. It gives shelter from the wind and showers, and

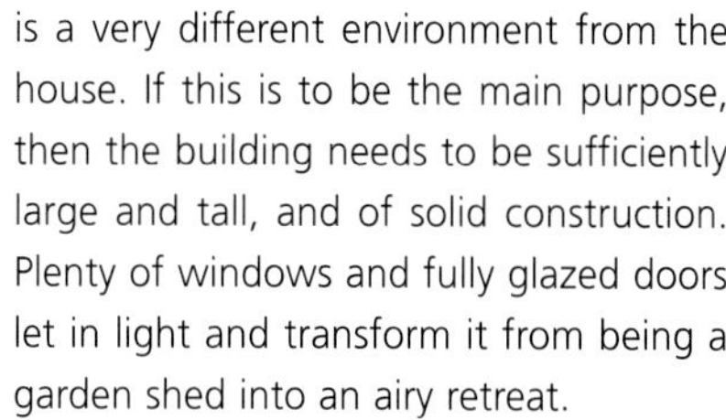

is a very different environment from the house. If this is to be the main purpose, then the building needs to be sufficiently large and tall, and of solid construction. Plenty of windows and fully glazed doors let in light and transform it from being a garden shed into an airy retreat.

Small summerhouses with only a few windows invariably end up as a storage shed for garden furniture and equipment. This can make them unsightly, and it is likely they won't be used as places to sit in. If this is a risk, and if you are choosing a summerhouse as a garden feature rather than a retreat, then an open gazebo is a safer and prettier choice.

Classic, simple designs are usually the best choice, painted in a pleasing neutral colour that is harmonious with the landscape: soft sage green, dark holly green and cream are all safe choices with surrounding foliage. Avoid summerhouses with a surfeit of timber decoration, as their appearance will probably seem fussy and out of place in the garden.

THE GARDEN SHED

Garden sheds provide essential storage space and, often, a bolt-hole for the handyman of the house. One thing is certain: they are never big enough. Before choosing, assess the future storage space requirements of the garden and the household: bicycles, garden furniture, camping equipment, household and garden tools and mowers. Buy a quality building that will last and look good in

TRANSFORMING STRUCTURES WITH COLOUR

Many new or existing timber garden structures can be transformed with a coat or two of wood colour. Arbours, summerhouses and gazebos are designed to be noticed, not concealed by planting. Choose a colour that suits the style of your garden and one that is in sympathy with surrounding plants. Green is the obvious choice, but it is often the hardest to get right. Select soft shades that are easy to live with and choose lighter colours for small spaces. Bright, bold colours suit sunny Mediterranean and coastal gardens with high light levels.

PLANNING PERMISSION

Most garden buildings are low enough and small enough not to require planning permission. In the case of larger summerhouses and home office buildings, certain authorities may impose planning requirements in some circumstances. If in doubt, contact your local authority planning department.

SHEDS: POINTS TO CONSIDER

- Windows facing the house are not a good idea: the contents of a shed are never an attractive feature.
- Double doors are a worthwhile consideration for those with large gardens and bulky garden equipment.
- It is worth considering the strength of the shed's floor. Inexpensive garden buildings compromise on the amount of support timbers used in the floor; this could be a problem when storing heavy equipment.
- When it comes to wood colourings and preservatives, choose a product that combines both. Dark wood colours are always best: they disappear into the garden and blend with the vegetation. Light, bright colours draw attention and will make a utility building into an unsightly feature.

This romantic ruin is a folly created as a focal point to fire the imagination. The visitor has to ask, What was it originally? Where was it ? And what was it used for?

the garden. Of course you can screen it, but deteriorating garden buildings are unsightly and cost maintenance time.

In smaller spaces, storage chests and wall stores are a useful way of incorporating storage space. Positioned against the wall of the house, or a wall or fence close to the building, they are not obtrusive and provide a valuable place to house garden equipment, boots, toys and furniture accessories. Some tall wall storage buildings can be made attractive by tasteful painting and planting, and take on the appearance of a doorway or other entrance into the garden. Some garden storage chests can double up as seating in the patio or courtyard.

THE HOME OFFICE

With developments in technology, more of us are working from home. There is pressure on space in most households; a separate building that can be used as a study or office is a real consideration. The garden can provide a wonderfully relaxing, light environment in which to work. High-quality buildings suitable for this purpose are in a different price league from the average shed or summerhouse, but they are an excellent investment where this space will be used. A power supply is essential, as is easy all-weather access and good insulation. The home office building is not only a consideration for larger gardens, where it can be 'lost' among other elements of the garden; modern buildings with clean lines and plenty of glass suit contemporary garden designs and can become a major part of the picture – an extension of the house separated by an open area of planting.

FOLLIES

A folly is a building constructed with the sole purpose of creating an illusion, a focal point in the landscape. In the era of grand gardens designed by landscapers such as 'Capability' Brown, follies often took the form of ancient and classical buildings designed to add romance and mystery to the picture and provoke questions and wonder from the garden visitor. Sham castles and ruins were popular, built far from the house to add an air of civilization to a landscape of grass and trees.

Follies are fun and are a possibility in gardens of today. In a large space, it is often difficult to find a garden building that is in keeping with an informal landscape and one that will create sufficient impact to draw the eye within a large picture. A stone folly, perhaps a ruin, is easily constructed from old brick, rendered blocks and reconstituted stone components. Individual touches can be added with pieces collected from reclamation yards. It is a certain way of achieving a completely individual garden ornament on a larger scale.

Garden features

Just as a room is brought to life by the addition of well-chosen accessories, for example pictures and ornaments, so is a garden enhanced by objects that reflect the taste and personality of the owner. Whatever the size of the garden, a few appropriate features such as pots, statues, structures and sculptures complete the picture by adding character and making it individual.

A classic stone urn and pedestal provide solid structure and a bold focal point amid a light, ethereal planting of silver, white and blue.

Objects are an excellent way to create a feel or accentuate a theme in the garden. A stone lantern transforms a bamboo, an acer and some gravel into a Japanese-style garden. A terracotta wall mask, a vine-draped pergola and a few gourds will turn a patio into a Mediterranean terrace. A meandering gravel path, some large pebbles and reed-like plants create the feeling of a river bed – add an old boat or the suggestion of a landing stage, and the picture is complete.

Features are also a useful way to draw the eye to one area rather than another. If there is something unsightly in the garden, a common tendency is to try and screen it. However, a permanent feature, such as a well-chosen statue or bold pot, or an urn or obelisk, draws the eye to an area of your choice and provides an attractive focal point around which you can concentrate the planting.

DESIGN AND SETTING

When choosing an ornament, select one that is appropriate to the location, and make sure the colour and texture of the materials used fit in with any other hard landscaping materials, such as the brick of the house and your local stone. Appropriateness is all-important. (See Choosing Materials, pages 62–63.) The secret of success is to stay simple and to choose a classic design. Never be influenced by the price of an ornament:

it is the design and the setting of the feature that are the keys to success.

A garden ornament provides a vital focal point, a punctuation mark amid a mass of stems and foliage. When positioning the feature, remember it is there to attract the eye, so place it where you want the centre of attention to be, and create the right surroundings to set it off. Birdbaths, sundials, statues and urns are often lost through poor positioning and the wrong setting. A sundial in the middle of the lawn will need to be an impressive structure to maintain its presence against the vast green sward. A birdbath perched on the edge of the patio will look hard and awkward without planting to soften it.

This beautifully simple stone pot is balanced and linked to the pool beside it by the striking architectural foliage of hostas and bergenias.

PERSONALIZE THE PLOT

You do not need to spend a fortune on garden ornaments. Nor do you have to go for the conventional sundial, birdbath or statue. Take a look around reclamation yards, junk shops and car boot sales, and you will find all sorts of artefacts that make wonderful garden features: old tools, metal watering cans, galvanized buckets, and even roof tiles. There are also many natural objects that

A decorative roof ridge tile, a pile of old terracotta flowerpots and a terracotta wall mask are all eye-catching features within the garden picture.

A handsome bird of prey carved from oak, which is a durable, natural alternative to stone: it weathers beautifully and also sits comfortably in an informal setting.

fulfil the role of garden ornaments: logs, driftwood, rocks, pebbles, shells and rope all tell a story. Use items that you have collected and perhaps hold memories for you, and group objects with a similar theme together, combining them with suitable plants in appropriate containers.

In a contemporary setting, wonderful sculpture can be created by using scrap metals and a pot of metal paint. In cottage and country gardens, the relics of gardens of the past add a sense maturity.

CHOOSING MATERIALS

Most stone garden ornaments start life as an original piece of sculpture or architectural masonry carved by a stone mason, either for use as a garden ornament or reclaimed from a building. A mould is made from this piece of stone and then others are cast in the mould from a mixture of stone dust and cement. The two methods of casting are known as slip-moulding and press-moulding. A slip-moulded ornament has a smooth, hard surface (lesser-quality castings may have pit marks, caused by bubbles in the mixture). The ornament or pot will be hardwearing and durable, but this type of material casts off moisture and the spores of moss and algae that give an object that weathered look. Press-moulded, reconstituted stone pieces weather well and mature quickly to an 'antique' finish, resembling original stone more closely than slip-moulded ornaments.

Original pieces are carved in quantity from granite in the Far East. These are an excellent choice for a garden with an oriental or contemporary theme, and work well in small spaces. Those of simpler design and without decoration tend to be the most enduringly pleasing.

Contemporary sculptures carved from sandstone and marble are popular and offer a smoother alternative to granite. Their clean lines and simplicity make them suitable for contemporary or coastal gardens, where they work well with water-washed pebbles. They need clever planting around them in other settings to blend them into the landscape.

These stone doves are made from press-moulded, reconstituted stone and will weather in the same way as an original stone carving.

Sculptures carved from hardwood, such as oak and teak, can be as long-lasting as stone and have a wonderfully organic character that works particularly well in naturalistic and rural settings. Birds and animals, both abstract and realistic, are popular subjects. Natural driftwood sculptures also work well in both contemporary courtyard settings and in large, open spaces. You have the satisfaction of knowing that every one is an individual and cannot be replicated.

Lead and bronze are classic materials for both traditional and contemporary garden sculpture. Lead is used for classical statuary, masks and containers; bronze or bronze resin is widely used for contemporary figures. Both materials are expensive but worth considering if the piece will be in a prominent position.

At flower shows and garden galleries, sculptors exhibit the garden antiques of tomorrow. These are often a good investment, but as the owner is going to live with his or her decision for many years, personal taste must be the main consideration. Security and insurance are worth a thought at this point.

GETTING THE SCALE RIGHT

The size of any ornament or feature in the garden needs to be in proportion to the area of the garden in which it is located and to the surrounding planting. A small space does not necessarily mean a small ornament if the planting is bold and there is room to stand back and view the piece from a distance. When choosing your feature, bear in mind that people often opt for pieces that are too small for their situation. This is because items invariably look considerably larger in a shop or garden centre than when situated in the space of a garden.

WATER FEATURES

The self-contained water feature has become a 'must-have' in small gardens in recent years. The sound and movement it contributes will bring a garden to life. Stone and terracotta features often come ready-equipped with pumps and need only the addition of water and a power supply. Pebble pools (left) utilize a sump, often sunk into the ground, and the water is circulated over stones. These are a safer way to incorporate water into a garden where there are children. They offer a low-maintenance alternative to the garden pond and are very useful in shaded gardens, where water plants struggle to thrive. Remember, any power supply must be installed by a qualified electrician.

GARDEN LIGHTING

Garden lighting will transform a garden after dark, creating a magical picture that can be enjoyed from the house at any time of the year. In summer it brings the night garden to life as a venue for dining and entertaining. Numerous low-voltage garden lighting kits are available that operate several lights off one transformer. These are good in small spaces, where the garden owner wants to experiment with light on a low budget. In larger spaces, and for a more permanent installation, a garden-lighting professional is the best option. Solar lighting is useful to provide subtle light to mark a path or steps; it will not illuminate a garden.

PLANTING

Paving, buildings, features and structures are all important elements of the design of an outdoor space, but it is the planting – the way plants are put together in terms of their shape, colour and texture – that makes the space a garden and gives it an identity. Plants change with the seasons, and different types of plants have their roles to play at different times of the year: trees create vertical interest and provide structure above eye level; shrubs create the framework of the garden in the middle layer of planting; and perennials, annuals and bulbs contribute seasonal colour in the foreground and add interest to the lower layer of the picture.

RIGHT: Exuberant planting in a summer garden.

What makes good planting?

A successfully planted garden has interest and variety throughout the year, and contains plants that play a variety of different roles – leading and supporting – on the garden stage. All the selected plants need to complement and contrast with others in the scheme, and should be in proportion to one another – the overall objective is to create a pleasing picture.

Good planting consists of a variety of plant form, colour and texture.

Early gardens were created using a limited range of plants, which were clipped and shaped to provide structure and variety of form. The parterre, the knot garden, topiary and hedges grew out of the gardener's desire to enclose space and create a picture from available plant material. These gardens were basically 'patterns' made from plants against the backdrop of the natural landscape, or in an enclosure surrounded by walls.

Variations on this type of garden endured throughout Europe until the Victorian era, when the introduction of a vast range of new garden plants collected from the far corners of the world by the plant hunters changed the catalogue of materials gardeners had to work with. Exotic and colourful blooms, a variety of leaf forms and textures, and different plant shapes flooded into gardens, filling them with variety.

As gardens developed and diversity increased, more and more hybrids and varieties came into being, and plants displaying exceptional qualities were nurtured and propagated by the gardener. For example variegated forms, which rarely occur in the wild and were highly prized, were selected and cultivated for gardens. It seems that the greater the variety of plants available, the greater was the gardeners' lust for more.

Today, the palette of plant material is bigger than ever before – the largest problem is knowing what to choose.

PLANTING FOR STRUCTURE

All gardens need structure: this is the enduring element of the garden that holds it together throughout the year, regardless of seasonal colour and interest. A sense of structure may be provided by walls, buildings, pergolas and arches (see pages 56–59), but it is most successfully achieved with plants. Trees (see pages 72–75), deciduous and evergreen shrubs (see pages 76–91) and conifers (see pages 76, 92–93) all provide permanent structure in the planting. Structural plants can be used formally or informally, according to the design of the garden, but they must be distributed throughout the planting to create a balanced picture.

Because the majority of garden trees are deciduous, evergreen shrubs are particularly important when it comes to providing structure. These can often be pruned or trimmed to retain a size and shape that is in proportion with the rest of the garden. They come into their own in the winter months, when deciduous shrubs lose their leaves and become a filigree framework.

PLANTS FOR TOPIARY *Buxus sempervirens* • × *Cupressocyparis leylandii* 'Castlewellan' • *Euonymus fortunei* • *Ilex crenata* •

CHOOSE A VARIETY OF PLANTS

An easy trap to fall into is to restrict yourself to plants that you are immediately drawn to and to ignore those that hold the show together. Herbaceous perennials may be your favourite group of plants, but most contribute little in the winter months. Evergreen shrubs may be easy to grow and require little attention, but most provide little colour in the summer. A well-planted garden contains a combination of different types of plant, each playing its own unique part in the garden scene.

The key to interesting planting is to include a diversity of plant shapes, foliage colours and textures. Small leaves help to lighten the heavy form of large, bold leaves (top left), and spiky plants are useful for adding emphasis among groups of soft, rounded subjects in the border (centre). Contrasting leaf colours are also striking (top right), and variegated foliage breaks up a mass of plain green.

STRUCTURAL PLANTING

As well as providing permanent interest, structural planting can also be used to achieve a degree of privacy from neighbouring properties. Hedges and screening shrubs are a dominant element in the structure of the garden: choose them well, and they will serve both purposes. A hedge may become superfluous if large, evergreen structure shrubs are planted in front of it. Doing away with the hedge would save room and dispense with the need for clipping.

Timescale is an important consideration. Some evergreens, such as **yew** (*Taxus,* see pages 76–77, 93) and **holly** (*Ilex,* pages 80, 91), make wonderful structure plants but will take several years to fulfil their role. This may be fine if you are looking at the garden as a long-term project, but for quicker results select a faster-growing alternative such as ***Pittosporum tenuifolium***♀ (see page 79).

PLANTING LAYERS

For an interesting, three-dimensional garden, try to include plants at various heights. The lower layer of planting, below eye level, is the easiest to add to, but do not ignore the layers above it – the middle and top layers, provided by trees and shrubs, are just as important. When choosing plants, consider their size and where they will fit in, as well as what they will contribute within that layer of the planting picture.

Laurus nobilis • *Ligustrum delavayanum* • *Lonicera nitida* 'Baggesen's Gold' • *Olea europaea* • *Taxus baccata* •

COLOURS AND THEIR EFFECTS

Yellow is a strong colour that attracts the eye. Use it where you want to draw attention: to highlight a focal point or to mark an entrance perhaps. If using it to lift a planting, then distribute it lightly and evenly, perhaps by incorporating a flower with a yellow centre.

White flowers are clean and fresh and stand out in the evening or in low light conditions. Combined with green flowers and foliage, white blooms create a cool, lush combination that is restful, pleasing, and easy to live with.

Abundant shades of green are always beneficial in the garden: they are relaxing in their own right, and dilute the impact of colours that do not sit happily together.

Soft pinks, mauves and blues are feminine shades that are gentle and work well in informal garden settings.

Strong reds and oranges are hot, exciting colours that demand attention; be certain that you can live with them before you include them in a prominent location or *en masse* in the garden.

Blue is the perfect mixer. It combines with virtually any other colour and it brings together colours that would not otherwise sit happily alongside one another. Blue works well in low light conditions and increases in depth and intensity at the beginning and end of the day.

THE IMPORTANCE OF COLOUR

There is great emphasis placed on the importance of colour in our lives: how we dress, how we decorate our homes, and how we plant our gardens. The influence of fashion changes how we think we should feel about colour, but personal taste is usually the strongest influence on what we choose. In the shorter term, our mood influences how we feel about colour, and certain colours can, it seems, have an effect on our moods.

Regardless of personal preference, the fact that some colours work together more successfully than others cannot be ignored. 'All colours go together in a garden' is an often-quoted saying. It is true to a certain extent, but when the gardener gets the combination of colours absolutely right, the effect can be particularly striking. The more open-minded the gardener can be, the greater the possibilities of appealing planting combinations. Sticking too strictly to a particular colour theme may exclude some very useful plants that would potentially be more successful than those you have chosen just for their colour.

There are certain rules that can be used as a guide to which colours work together and which ones do not. However, the eye of the gardener must direct the decision. Larger gardens are able to accommodate a wider colour range than small spaces.

LIME-GREEN PLANTS TO LIFT A BORDER *Alchemilla mollis* • *Bupleurum fruticosum* • *Cephalaria gigantea* •

A powerful colour theme using the yellow foliage of *Cornus alba* 'Aurea', the gold-variegated leaves of *Euonymus* 'Emerald 'n' Gold' and the acid-green flowers of *Euphorbia characias*.

COLOUR THEMING

It is never easy to maintain a colour theme in a border throughout the year: it demands careful planning for continuity of colour. A colour theme is more easily sustained if foliage is used to hold the theme together (see box, right). A yellow border is easily created in this way using gold foliage plants and those with yellow-variegated foliage: the colour theme is already there before seasonal yellow flowers are added. The addition of yellow tulips in spring, lupins in early summer, heleniums and rudbeckias in late summer, dahlias in autumn and witch hazel (*Hamamelis*) and mahonia in winter will complete the picture.

If the plan is to maintain a specific colour theme in a border throughout much of the year, it is advisable to leave gaps that can be filled with bulbs and annuals of the appropriate colour to maintain the theme.

THE IMPORTANCE OF FOLIAGE

When planning a colour-themed planting, consider the colour of the foliage as well as the flowers (see also pages 96–103).

Yellow- and gold-variegated foliage works well with a yellow or orange scheme.

Silver, grey and blue foliage links a scheme with blue-flowered subjects.

Plum foliage binds reds, pinks and purples, and also works as a background for hot oranges and warm yellows.

Leaves with white variegations look superb in a scheme with white-flowered plants, in sun or shade.

Digitalis lutea • *Euphorbia palustris* • *Heuchera* 'Key Lime Pie' • *Nicotiana* 'Lime Green' • *Smyrnium perfoliatum* •

ALTERING THE BALANCE

Soft colour combinations can be made livelier and richer by introducing darker shades in the form of flowers or foliage. For example, the deep burgundy foliage of *Lysimachia ciliata* 'Firecracker'♀ (see page 99) or the rich ruby blooms of *Cirsium rivulare* 'Atropurpureum' will add depth to a planting of soft pinks, lilacs and blues. Lime-green flowers and foliage, such as those of *Alchemilla mollis*♀ (see page 106), will lift any planting scheme.

If one colour looks out of place in a planting scheme it may be made acceptable by adding more of the same elsewhere in the planting to create a balanced picture. For example, one yellow foliage shrub may stand as the odd man out, but by adding other yellow foliage plants and yellow flowers it may look more comfortable and intended.

The vibrant flowers of *Euphorbia griffithii* 'Fireglow' are intensified against the plum foliage of *Acer palmatum* var. *dissectum* 'Crimson Queen'.

By grouping plants together that perform at the same time of the year their impact is increased and the interest is concentrated in one area of the garden.

SEASONAL COLOURS

Seasonal colours – those that predominate at a certain time of the year – rarely look out of place in the garden. Pale yellows and blues in early spring work with fresh, light green foliage. In summer, pinks, blues and lavender suit the warm days. Red, orange, gold and burgundy are the shades of autumn. In winter, the subtle colours of stems, evergreen leaves and delicate flowers stand out without the dilution of the heavy green of summer leaves. (See also pages 104–109.)

By grouping plants together that excel in a particular season, the interest for a certain time of the year is concentrated in a specific area of the garden: it is then easier to get the combination of colours right in that plant group. For example, a hot spot for late summer could include dahlias, cannas, heleniums and crocosmias. At another time of the year, an adjacent spot could include a totally different theme for a different time of the year: perhaps a softer combination for early summer containing blue nepeta, pink roses and purple alliums. The blue nepeta may go on flowering but will still mix with the hot colours of late summer. Generally, the most successful colour combinations are achieved in plant groupings rather than in entire colour-themed beds.

PLANTS WITH FEATHERY FOLIAGE *Actaea simplex* Atropurpurea Group • *Anthriscus sylvestris* 'Ravenswing' •

CREATE A FEELING OF SPACE

In a small, enclosed garden, a simple, light colour scheme will create a feeling of space. However, to make the planting interesting and to hold attention you need to use a wide variety of shades and different textures. Very simple planting can be striking, but it can be dull if there is not sufficient diversity.

Colour can also be used to draw attention to points in a space, and to emphasize or soften a boundary. If you use light colours at the end of a garden it can demarcate the boundary, drawing attention to where the garden ends. If darker colours are used in the same place, the far boundary is more likely to blend and fade into the surroundings, making the garden appear larger.

The spiky leaves of *Glyceria maxima* var. *variegata* and *Miscanthus sinensis* contrast with the bold foliage of *Hosta* 'Francee' and the structural seedheads of *Angelica archangelica*.

The lovely blooms of *Tulipa* 'Temple of Beauty' with the delicate foliage of *Acer palmatum*.

TEXTURE AND FORM

A variety of different plant forms and textures is just as important as colour in a planting scheme. Soft, rounded plant forms need the contrast of vertical shapes and spiky foliage to bring them to life. Bold leaves and blooms stand out against a backdrop of soft, feathery foliage.

Because different textures reflect light in different ways, they alter the appearance of leaves in varying light conditions. This is well illustrated in a planting of green foliage that includes a wide range of plant forms and textures: the diversity of colours and hues and interest in the planting can be just as great as in one incorporating a wide variety of contrasting colours.

In planning a scheme, aim for a variety of plant shapes, foliage shapes and sizes and textures. Include some plants that provide vertical emphasis and spiky leaves such as grasses, irises, sisyrinchiums and phormiums. Use some of these in the foreground to give depth to the planting. Also, include some with large leaves, such as bergenias and hostas, and those with smaller, softer leaves, such as herbaceous geraniums. Combine glossy leaves with soft, feathery foliage, and simple leaves with more intricate shapes.

Artemisia absinthium 'Lambrook Silver' • *Foeniculum vulgare* 'Purpureum' • *Perovskia* 'Blue Spire' •

Trees

The tree canopy occupies the highest level of planting, above eye level. Without this, a garden is too flat – a two-dimensional pattern of plants and lawn without height and scale. As well as providing interest in terms of colour and form, trees also bring about subtle changes in light conditions and can alter the perspective of the garden.

Any garden, however small, should include at least one tree. Light, airy trees, such as **birch** (*Betula*), **mountain ash** (*Sorbus*) and **alder** (*Alnus*), are ideal in smaller gardens, and provide vertical structure, movement and light, dappled shade. They are also good for underplanting. Fastigiate trees, such as

Fagus sylvatica 'Dawyck Purple'

Carpinus betulus 'Fastigiata' grows broader with age but retains its upright habit.

THE BEST TIME TO PLANT TREES

Autumn is the traditional time for planting. The soil is moist and warm, and deciduous plants are entering their dormant season. Beneath the ground, roots stay active and newly planted trees have the whole winter to get established before they have leaves and flowers to support next spring. Although container-growing has made it possible to plant any time, autumn is still the best season to plant large shrubs and trees.

Fagus sylvatica **'Dawyck Purple'♀** and ***Carpinus betulus*** **'Fastigiata'♀**, form dense columns, often clothed to the ground. If trimmed as standards, they have a tall, narrow head and cast little shade; they also provide dramatic height. The compact-headed, upright ***Pyrus calleryana*** **'Chanticleer'♀** does a similar job. (See page 146.)

TREES WITH SPRING BLOSSOM

About 20 years ago the most popular choices for garden trees were flowering cherries (*Prunus*), ornamental crab apples (*Malus*) and laburnums. Although spectacular in flower, many of these have a relatively short season of interest. However, for those who crave spring blossom, *Prunus* 'Accolade'♀ is a good choice; it is a small tree of light, spreading habit; the profuse rich pink flowers appear in early spring, and they are weather-resistant and last well. *Prunus* 'Ukon'♀ (1) flowers in mid-spring and is a good alternative to the sugar pink and white of most cherries. It is a medium-sized, spreading tree with bronze new foliage – a lovely setting for the pale cream to green, semi-double flowers. It benefits from good autumn foliage colour, the leaves turning deep reddish-purple.

Ornamental varieties of crab apples, such as *Malus* 'John Downie'♀ and *Malus* × *zumi* var. *calocarpa* 'Golden Hornet'♀ (2), have attractive apple blossom, followed by fruits in autumn (see page 151). One of the best is *Malus* 'Evereste'♀, with dark pink flower buds opening to profuse pure white flowers followed by yellow-orange fruits. It has a neat, conical habit, making it an excellent structure tree for the smaller garden.

Crataegus laevigata 'Paul's Scarlet'♀ (3) is one of the loveliest hawthorns for gardens, with a spreading head of fresh green leaves. The branches are garlanded with a mass of double scarlet flowers in late spring, after most other spring blossom has faded. It grows well on chalk and clay and suits country gardens.

WHAT SIZE OF TREE TO PLANT?

When choosing a tree, the temptation is to save time by planting as large a specimen as possible. Bare-root, open-ground plants are often larger than container-grown trees, but they may take more time to establish, and growth in the first couple of seasons may be slow or negligible. Although container-grown plants are generally smaller, they will suffer little transplanting check and, provided they are given adequate care after planting, should grow quickly in the first season. Some types of tree are notoriously difficult to establish from bare-root stock, namely the tulip tree (*Liriodendron*), walnut (*Juglans*), sweet gum (*Liquidambar*) and birch (*Betula*).

Catalpa bignonioides 'Aurea'

Amelanchier lamarckii

MULTI-SEASONAL TREES

In smaller gardens, where there is space for only one or two trees, it is important to select varieties that work hard to earn their space. Trees grown for their colourful foliage look good throughout spring, summer and autumn. For example, *Catalpa bignonioides* 'Aurea'🏆 (golden Indian bean tree) is a striking plant with very large, velvety yellow leaves becoming yellow-green as summer progresses. White foxglove-like flowers appear on mature plants. Its exotic appearance works well in contemporary schemes, and it is effective grown in a large container near the house, where its bold form is balanced by the building. The one disadvantage of catalpa is its lateness to break into leaf. However, its branch framework is interesting and architectural. (See also page 112.)

Amelanchier lamarckii🏆 is glorious in spring, when it explodes into a cloud of starry white flowers and soft, coppery leaves. A small, bushy tree with a spreading head, it colours well in autumn. Although usually recommended for neutral to acid soil, it succeeds on alkaline soils.

Betula utilis var. *jacquemontii*

Some trees, such as ***Betula utilis* var. *jacquemontii***, have attractive bark. The white trunk and branches of this Himalayan birch are striking against the green of the foliage in summer and outstanding when further exposed in winter. The fine twigs of the birch create a dark filigree against the winter sky and are hung with golden brown catkins in early spring. (See page 141.) The cultivar ***Betula utilis* var. *jacquemontii* 'Silver Shadow'**🏆 is smaller-growing, and has dazzling white stems. It is well worth considering for medium-sized gardens.

Some **dogwood** (*Cornus*) cultivars are excellent choices for smaller gardens. They are extremely hardy, and although ideal in woodland gardens, they are surprisingly easy to accommodate in more contemporary settings. They prefer neutral to acid soil, and are not suited to shallow soils over chalk. The cultivars of ***Cornus florida*** form a bushy, conical tree of stiff but elegant habit. The beautiful petal-like bracts adorn the branches in late spring, and the leaves colour richly in autumn. ***Cornus florida* 'Cherokee Chief'**🏆 is a superb form, with deep rose-red bracts. ***Cornus* 'Porlock'**🏆 (see pages 7, 140) is a graceful, small spreading tree with semi-evergreen leaves. The flowerheads have creamy-white bracts in late spring that turn rich pink in early summer. These are followed by strawberry-like fruits that hang from the branches in autumn.

Evergreen trees are few in number, hence the popularity of the fast-growing **eucalyptus**. Many get rather too large

SECRETS OF SUCCESS WITH NEW TREES

Success with newly planted trees depends on secure staking, sound soil preparation, good planting compost, and thorough watering through the first year. Tree ties should secure the tree firmly without damaging the bark and restricting the flow of sap. If deer and rabbits are a problem, use substantial tree guards to protect the trunk, as damage can be fatal.

MORE COMPACT TREES FOR SMALL GARDENS *Albizia julibrissin* f. *rosea* • *Crataegus persimilis* 'Prunifolia' •

rather too quickly. ***Eucalyptus pauciflora* subsp. *niphophila***♀ (snow gum) is smaller and a good choice for a medium-sized garden. (See also page 120.)

Some of the ornamental **cherries** have beautiful bark, a much longer-lasting attribute than their short-lived flowers. ***Prunus serrula***♀ is the most striking, with polished mahogany bark from an early age. The leaves are small and narrow and the white flowers are insignificant, but if the surrounding planting is designed to enhance the stem of the tree it is a good choice. ***Prunus maackii* 'Amber Beauty'** has an upright, narrow habit and white flowerheads that resemble those of *Prunus laurocerasus*♀ (cherry laurel, see page 77). The stem is amber-coloured, smooth and very beautiful, especially when rising from ferns and grasses.

Sorbus aucuparia var. *xanthocarpa*

There are many varieties of **sorbus** to choose from: those with fern-like foliage and those with large, rounded, often silvery leaves. ***Sorbus commixta* 'Embley'**♀ is a superb small mountain ash with fern-like leaves that colour scarlet in autumn. The white flowers in spring are followed by heavy bunches of orange-red berries. ***Sorbus* 'Joseph Rock'** is similar in stature, with an upright head, amber-yellow fruits and spectacular autumn colour (see page 151). Berrying sorbus are a good choice if you want to attract birds into the garden in late autumn and early winter. The yellow- and white-berried varieties, for example ***Sorbus aucuparia* var. *xanthocarpa***♀ tend to hold on to their berries for longer before the birds finally strip the branches.

TREES IN POTS

Many smaller trees can be grown in containers, enabling height to be introduced into any area of the garden. Growing a tree in a pot will restrict its size without impairing its performance if a large container and properly formulated compost are used. Controlled-release fertilizer should be added twice a year, and regular watering is essential. The ultimate size of the tree will be restricted by the size of the pot but this need not impact on its performance. Good subjects for containers include *Catalpa bignonioides* 'Aurea'♀, *Acer palmatum* varieties (above) and *Cornus* 'Porlock'♀.

Eucalyptus pauciflora subsp. *niphophila*

Prunus serrula

Koelreuteria paniculata • *Prunus* × *blireana* • *Prunus* 'Spire' • *Pyrus salicifolia* 'Pendula' • *Sorbus hupehensis* •

A standard bay (*Laurus nobilis*) adds height to a formal design of trimmed box (*Buxus sempervirens*).

Evergreen shrubs for structure

Evergreen shrubs that provide essential structure in the garden come in a variety of shapes and sizes. The broad-leaved evergreens of the Victorian shrubbery may well come to mind – and they do have a role to play – but there are structure evergreens that have smaller, lighter leaves, which provide a contrast to bolder, broader foliage. Variegated shrubs (see pages 96–97) and flowering evergreens (see pages 84–85) are also an integral part of the structure of the garden, introducing colour and variety.

Conifers contribute plant shapes and foliage effects that differ from those of broad-leaved evergreens. ***Taxus baccata***♀ (yew) is perhaps the ultimate structure plant, grown for its dark foliage, the characteristic forms of its cultivars, and the ability of the species to be trimmed and shaped into a great variety of living masonry. It is considered a long-term prospect in the garden; however, if planted young on fertile soil it can grow quite quickly. Yew hedges are normally grown from seed-raised stock that will show some variety in form and colour, a variation that is usually lost with maturity and clipping if they are trained as a hedge. Yew is the ultimate hedge for either a traditional or a contemporary setting; its dark, raven-green hue is quite different from most other greens in the garden.

Also consider growing yew as individual trimmed or lightly shaped specimens. It will easily make a narrow or broad cone that looks good manicured (see page 93) or allowed a more informal appearance. Grown like this, it can be used to provide height among plantings of low shrubs, especially woody aromatics and silver foliage subjects. It will also give weight

PLANTING A YEW HEDGE

Conifer hedges are best planted in autumn, while the soil is still warm and moist. Container-grown plants will establish quickly but will only be available up to 60cm (2ft) or so high. Larger stock of 60–90cm (2–3ft) will be field-grown and lifted with a rootball. Bare-root stock is not a good choice for yew. Plant 1m (40in) apart (taking the distance from the centre of one plant to another) in well-prepared soil, and top-dress with a general slow-release fertilizer. Yew often produces long, irregular growth at the top of the plant; light trimming from an early age in late spring or early summer will encourage bushy growth.

GOOD SCREENING PLANTS *Cotoneaster franchetii* • *Elaeagnus* × *ebbingei* • *Escallonia rubra* 'Crimson Spire' •

and permanent structure in formal and informal herbaceous plantings.

Some forms of yew naturally grow into bold, architectural shapes. ***Taxus baccata*** **'Fastigiata'**🏆 develops into a dark green column up to 4m (12ft) high, sometimes studded with waxy red fruits. The hybrid ***Taxus* × *media*** **'Hicksii'**🏆 forms a broad column of dark green; a female clone, it also has the added advantage of bearing red berries.

Buxus sempervirens🏆 (common box) is another structure classic. The species is used to create hedges and topiary (see also page 132), and left to grow it will develop into a large, handsome shrub up to 4m (12ft) or more in height. The dwarf box ***Buxus sempervirens*** **'Suffruticosa'**🏆 is used for dwarf hedges (up to 45cm/18in high) around formal beds and in parterres (see page 80). Both make excellent subjects to create bold green shapes in pots. The mid-green, matt, small, neat foliage of box is the perfect foil for other flowers and leaves. Some *Buxus sempervirens* cultivars have attractive cream variegations, for example ***Buxus sempervirens*** **'Elegantissima'**🏆; they work well when combined with green box and also make good variegated shrubs in their own right.

Laurus nobilis🏆 (sweet bay) is used extensively for trimming and training into cones, balls, lollipops and twisted stems. Trimmed and trained bays suit pots and containers in classic settings and town gardens. They are not plants for cold, exposed gardens and need sympathetic trimming and pinching of the new growth in spring to keep them in shape. A Mediterranean plant, bay is tolerant of dry conditions, so will cope with some neglect. If left to grow, it will develop into a large, broad, conical shrub with upward-sweeping branches and matt, dark green foliage. It is an excellent screening shrub. In milder areas it works well with the silver foliage of the olive ***Olea europaea***.

Taxus baccata

Buxus sempervirens 'Elegantissima'

Prunus laurocerasus

Prunus laurocerasus🏆 (cherry laurel), which has long been popular, is still widely planted. Its broad green, shiny leaves are appealing, and a well-maintained laurel hedge is a wonderful backdrop to planting. It grows quickly, which is part of its appeal. The disadvantage is that laurel is very greedy, draining the soil of water and nutrients, so it needs plenty of space around it. If grown as a hedge, trimming is laborious as it is best done with pruners rather than shears or a trimmer: partly cut leaves are not attractive.

Prunus lusitanica🏆 (Portugal laurel) is an excellent structure plant grown as a hedge or an individual specimen trimmed or allowed to develop its natural form. It has dark green, shiny leaves on red leaf stalks and a compact habit. If left to grow naturally, it forms a broad conical shrub up to 3m (10ft) or more in ten years, before developing into a handsome small tree. If lightly trimmed, it will give the effect of a topiary cone and, unlike yew, it grows well in a pot. This is a better choice than most for shallow chalk soils and dry conditions.

Griselinia littoralis • *Photinia* × *fraseri* 'Red Robin' • *Phyllostachys aurea* • *Pittosporum tenuifolium* • *Thuja plicata* •

DARKER, DENSER EVERGREENS

Aucubas are excellent evergreen structure shrubs for shade and are tolerant of poor soil, chalk and clay. They are ideal in city gardens and cope with atmospheric pollution. Most popular aucubas are variegated, such as *Aucuba japonica* 'Variegata', shown above (1). However, the dark green *Aucuba japonica* 'Rozannie'♀ is just as striking. Broad, dark leaves are carried on a rounded bush, which is rarely more than 1.5m (5ft) high and is the perfect setting for large red berries in winter.

Osmanthus × *burkwoodii*♀ is a compact shrub, often upright in habit when young. It matures to a large bush, up to 3m (10ft) high, but is easily maintained at half this size. Light brown stems carry very dark green leaves and fragrant white flowers in late spring. It is a hardy, tolerant shrub that makes an excellent plant for the back of a border. (See Good Companions, opposite.)

The variegated forms of *Osmanthus heterophyllus* are widely planted but the species is often overlooked as a useful evergreen and an alternative to *Ilex aquifolium*♀. It is slow-growing and good in shade, so suits a small garden. *Osmanthus heterophyllus* 'Purpureus' (2) has purple-tinged young growth and is a good choice for a border where space is limited.

Pittosporum tobira♀ (3) has long been used as a hedging and structure shrub in warmer regions. With milder winters, it is now more widely planted, especially in town gardens. The whorled arrangement of the leaves and their interesting oval, round-ended shape is most attractive. *Pittosporum tobira* responds well to pruning but left untrimmed will make a superb rounded shrub up to 3m (10ft) or more. In summer, deliciously fragrant flowers are produced in clusters at the end of the branches. They open white and age to rich cream. This shrub is very drought-resistant and grows in shade as well as in full sun.

FAST-GROWING STRUCTURE SHRUBS

Classic structure shrubs such as box (*Buxus,* pages 76, 80) and yew (*Taxus,* pages 77, 93) take considerable time to mature, and some gardeners may be too impatient to wait. There are, however, a number of good alternatives that grow quickly and provide evergreen structure in the garden in a fraction of the time.

Photinia × *fraseri* 'Red Robin'♀ (see Good Companions, opposite) is deservedly popular, with its shiny green leaves and bright red new growth. If lightly pruned in late spring and again in late summer it retains its scarlet new shoots for most of the year. Broad and upright in habit, it quickly attains a height of 3m (10ft). Its white flowers in spring and bright foliage will attract attention in the garden, so bear this in mind. It makes an excellent background plant for a scheme of hot colours but will overpower pastel shades.

Photinia × *fraseri* 'Red Robin'

Pittosporum tenuifolium♀ and its cultivars (see pages 83, 99) have smaller leaves than 'Red Robin', and fine dark stems. The species quickly grows to a tall, broad column of 4m (12ft) or more. The shiny light green leaves are gently waved and reflect the light to give a silvery effect in bright sunlight. The variegated forms, for example *Pittosporum* 'Garnettii'♀ (see page 99) and *Pittosporum tenuifolium* 'Gold Star', are useful to lighten other heavier screening evergreen shrubs, such as *Prunus laurocerasus*♀ (see page 77).

PRICKLY SHRUBS FOR SECURITY *Berberis darwinii* • *Berberis julianae* • *Genista hispanica* • *Hippophae rhamnoides* •

LIGHTER, AIRIER EVERGREENS

Evergreen structure shrubs with a lighter, more open habit are useful to provide a variety of texture in the planting scheme. They often suit rural situations better than more solid subjects.

Berberis × stenophylla♀ (1) is a graceful, arching shrub with narrow, dark green leaves and abundant spines. Its gentle habit belies its tough character. In late spring the branches are wreathed with soft orange-yellow flowers. (See Good Companions, below.)

Cotoneaster franchetii (2) is a light, arching shrub reaching about 2m (6ft). It has pretty, small sage green leaves and orange fruit in autumn. Its soft colour mixes well with deciduous shrubs, roses and perennials, and it grows on any soil.

Phillyrea angustifolia (3) deserves wider planting. Forming a soft, rounded shrub, 2m (6ft) in height, it has an abundance of narrow, shining green leaves. Small fragrant flowers – an added bonus – appear in the leaf axils in late spring and early summer. *Phillyrea latifolia* has broader shining green leaves and is larger-growing. Again, it has arching branches and a mass of foliage.

Pittosporum tenuifolium

GOOD COMPANIONS

The pale gold leaves of *Cornus alba* 'Aurea' (1) look good with the dark foliage and bright flowers of *Berberis × stenophylla*♀ (2). In winter, the red stems of the cornus are particularly striking.

The variegated *Euonymus fortunei* 'Emerald Gaiety'♀ (3) contrasts with the dark-leaved *Osmanthus × burkwoodii*♀ (4). The white osmanthus flowers highlight the euonymus's silver-white variegations.

The reddish flower buds of *Viburnum tinus* SPIRIT ('Anvi') (5) pick up the red buds and growth tips of *Photinia × fraseri* 'Red Robin'♀ (6). The leaves form a good contrast: dark and matt, light and glossy.

Ilex aquifolium • *Pyracantha* 'Orange Charmer' • *Rosa rugosa* • *Rubus cockburnianus* • *Ulex europaeus* •

Small evergreen shrubs

Small evergreen shrubs are among the most useful characters in the garden. They suit the narrow borders that exist in so many gardens, provide winter interest at the front of a border, and are ideal for permanent planting in containers. Many small evergreens are good in shade, and they are the ideal subjects to fill gloomy corners where colourful flowers will not grow. Their greatest attribute is that they stay compact and controllable, and pruning is rarely, if ever, required.

A parterre of *Buxus sempervirens* 'Suffruticosa' at Bourton House Garden, Bourton-on-the-Hill, Gloucestershire.

Box predominates as the most widely planted of all the dwarf evergreens. ***Buxus sempervirens* 'Suffruticosa'**♀ is ideal as dwarf hedges around beds of herbs and flowers and in parterres. Individual specimens make simple, easy-to-control topiary subjects in pots. ***Buxus microphylla* 'Faulkner'** has brighter, shinier foliage and a more horizontal growth habit. It is an excellent choice for trimming into classic box balls. Box grows in sun or shade.

Also good in sun or shade is ***Ilex crenata* 'Convexa'**♀, a form of the Japanese holly. It is a superb rounded, bushy dwarf evergreen growing up to 75cm (30in) or so in height. Its small, dark green leathery leaves are rounded and convex, adding to the solid, rounded character of the shrub. Good as a low hedge, this is an ideal plant to end a border with, or to repeat along a narrow bed in a formal scheme.

Ilex crenata 'Convexa'

MAINTAINING BOX SHAPES

Box balls, cones and spirals can be grown in the open ground and in pots. In containers and on well-drained soil they are susceptible to nutrient deficiency, because potash and nitrogen are washed from the soil during watering. This manifests itself as a light bronzing of the foliage and is particularly obvious in winter. As a preventive, apply a controlled-release fertilizer twice a year, in early spring and late summer. Trim box shapes after the first flush of growth in late spring and again in late summer, but not later than autumn. New growth is occasionally damaged by late frosts. Affected shoots can be trimmed off the shrubs and they quickly recover.

EVERGREEN GROUND COVER *Ceanothus* 'Centennial' • *Cotoneaster dammeri* • *Cotoneaster salicifolius* 'Gnom' •

Euonymus fortunei 'Emerald 'n' Gold'

Mahonia aquifolium 'Apollo'

Skimmia × confusa 'Kew Green'

SHRUBS FOR SHADE

The variegated forms of ***Euonymus fortunei*** are widely planted; they have a loose, spreading habit and are excellent in shade. For an even more compact plant, choose a variety of *Euonymus japonicus*. ***Euonymus japonicus* 'Microphyllus'**, with its upright green stems and closely packed, small shiny leaves, is similar in appearance to box. The variegated forms are particularly attractive, and are useful to brighten ground-cover plantings of vinca and ivy (*Hedera*) in shady corners. (See Good Companions, below.)

***Mahonia aquifolium* 'Apollo'** has bolder, holly-like foliage on suckering stems reaching 60cm (2ft) or so in height. The foliage is dark green but tends to flush burgundy in winter. This provides a marvellous background to the clusters of bright yellow flowers in spring. (See Good Companions, below.)

Also for shadier areas of the garden, ***Sarcococca confusa***♀ and other varieties of Christmas box are accommodating dwarf evergreens. They have suckering stems and eventually develop into dense upright shrubs. ***Sarcococca hookeriana* var. *digyna***♀ is taller, growing to 70cm (28in) or more, with narrow dark green leaves and purplish stems. (See Good Companions, left.) All sarcococcas have the bonus of small, pink-white fragrant flowers in winter.

Skimmias are always popular, grown for their winter buds, berries and fragrant flowers set against shiny evergreen foliage. Although those that berry are attractive, some of the male clones are even better, and are more reliable. ***Skimmia × confusa* 'Kew Green'**♀ is an excellent choice, forming a 1m (40in) mound of olive-green foliage smothered in large clusters of greenish buds in winter, opening into creamy fragrant flowers in spring. ***Skimmia japonica* 'Fragrans'**♀ is similar, with dense clusters of white flowers with a delicious lily-of-the-valley fragrance. ***Skimmia japonica* 'Rubella'**♀ is the most widely planted of all skimmias, with its dark leaves and red buds opening into pinkish-white flowers in spring. All skimmias prefer shade; their foliage tends to yellow in sun.

GOOD COMPANIONS

The tiny, golden-edged leaves of the dense *Euonymus japonicus* 'Microphyllus Pulchellus' (1) reflect the gold-centred leaves of the light, spreading *Vinca minor* 'Illumination' (2).

The dark green leaves and arching stems of *Sarcococca hookeriana* var. *digyna*♀ (3) are handsome set against the soft green and cream rosettes of *Pachysandra terminalis* 'Variegata'♀ foliage (4).

The gold-variegated leaves of *Euonymus fortunei* 'Emerald 'n' Gold'♀ (5) pick up the yellow in the spring flowers of *Mahonia aquifolium* 'Apollo'♀ (6) and contrast with the mahonia's dark foliage.

Hedera colchica • *Juniperus horizontalis* • *Pachysandra terminalis* • *Rubus tricolor* • *Vinca major* • *Vinca minor* •

Cistus × *purpureus*

SUN-LOVING SHRUBS

For sunny situations, **sun roses** (*Cistus*) deliver a spectacular display of white or pink flowers in early summer, in addition to providing mounds of evergreen foliage. Those with smaller leaves, for example ***Cistus* × *obtusifolius* 'Thrive'**, have a denser, more compact habit than those with larger leaves. Most form a low mound up to 1m (40in) or so in height, depending on the variety. The widely planted, hardy ***Cistus* × *hybridus*** grows larger and its vigour is often underestimated as it quickly reaches over 1m (40in) or so high and more across. ***Cistus* × *dansereaui* 'Decumbens'**🏆 is lower and spreading in habit. ***Cistus* × *purpureus***🏆 has a more open habit, with wavy-edged, dark green leaves and large, deep pink, maroon-blotched flowers.

The dwarf **hebes** continue to be popular because of their habit, attractive foliage and summer flowers. The tiny, bright green foliage and rounded form of ***Hebe* 'Emerald Gem'**🏆 brightens up any planting scheme and is particularly good with yellow flowers and golden variegations. Growing to only 30cm (12in), it is ideal surrounded by gravel and combines well with dwarf conifers.

The whipcord hebes are conifer-like plants, with tiny leaves flattened against their stems. They are valued for their highly unusual, seaweed-like appearance. ***Hebe ochracea* 'James Stirling'**🏆 has ochre-gold, cord-like foliage and stems and develops into a loose, star-shaped shrub up to 30cm (12in) high and more across. It combines well with the plum-coloured foliage of heucheras (see pages 83, 99) and the rich gold variegation of *Euonymus fortunei* 'Emerald 'n' Gold'🏆 (see page 81).

The silver-grey foliage hebes are superb shrubs for sunny situations and work well with other silver foliage shrubs, such as **santolina** and **helichrysum**. ***Hebe pinguifolia* 'Pagei'**🏆 is a classic, forming wide mats of blue-grey leaves. ***Hebe pimeleoides* 'Quicksilver'**🏆 is similar in colour but with a more open habit and smaller leaves. The newer introduction, ***Hebe* 'Clear Skies'**, has much brighter, bluer foliage. If a low, rounded bush is required rather than a broad mat, choose ***Hebe pinguifolia* 'Sutherlandii'**.

Hebe albicans🏆 and the hybrids derived from it are the best of the dwarf hebes to grow as low structure shrubs. Their upright stems, healthy foliage and

Hebe 'Red Edge'

SMALL EVERGREENS FOR POTS *Berberis* × *stenophylla* 'Corallina Compacta' • *Buxus microphylla* 'Faulkner' •

Pittosporum tenuifolium 'Tom Thumb'

Rosmarinus officinalis 'Severn Sea'

compact habit keep them looking good in the garden for several seasons. *Hebe albicans* is extremely hardy and is a useful soft celadon-green colour. ***Hebe* 'Red Edge'**♀ has greyer foliage, tinged purple at the tips and becoming much redder and quite striking in the winter months. It looks good planted in groups where it makes a rolling mound – a low-level cloud effect. (See Good Companions, below.)

The handsome ***Pittosporum tenuifolium* 'Tom Thumb'**♀ forms a dense, rounded, evergreen cone, up to 1m (40in) high, of dark, shining burgundy foliage in winter; its colour intensifies as the days get colder. In spring it is studded with bright green new growth. It is an excellent plant to bring depth of colour to sunny situations, for planting in gravel, or to combine with dwarf conifers and grasses; it is also an excellent subject for a pot. (See Good Companions, left.)

GOOD COMPANIONS

The soft, matt grey-purple foliage of *Salvia officinalis* 'Purpurascens'♀ (1) forms a beautiful contrast in texture planted with the harder, shinier dark leaves of *Pittosporum tenuifolium* 'Tom Thumb'♀ (2).

The pointed leaves and blue flowers of *Rosmarinus officinalis* 'Severn Sea'♀ (3) are a pretty partner for the tiny silver leaves and soft mounded form of the thyme *Thymus vulgaris* 'Silver Posie' (4).

The softly waved, dark plum leaves of *Heuchera* 'Plum Pudding' (5) form a contrast with the stiff, regular growth of *Hebe* 'Red Edge'♀ (6). The hebe's leaves are flushed purple-red in winter.

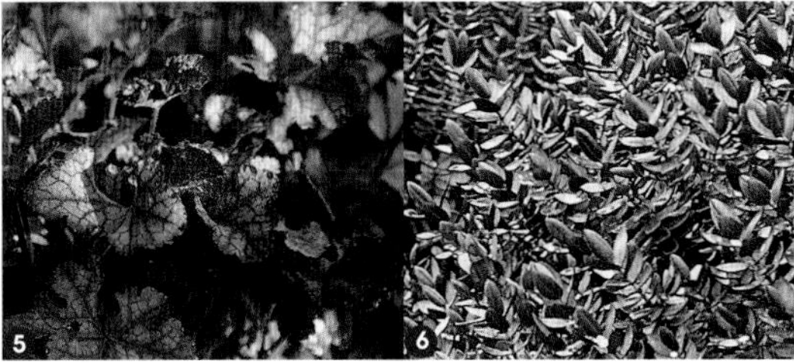

Salvia officinalis 'Purpurascens'

Rosmarinus officinalis (common rosemary) can make a larger shrub up to 2m (6ft) high. However, if picked or trimmed regularly it will normally form an upright bush up to half that height. The lovely ***Rosmarinus officinalis* 'Severn Sea'**♀ has a more relaxed habit: arching branches carry silver-green foliage and a mass of brilliant blue flowers in early spring. It forms a mound rarely more than 80cm (32in) in height. (See Good Companions, left.)

***Salvia officinalis* 'Purpurascens'**♀ is only evergreen in milder areas. In winter it is soft grey-purple, and in spring the new leaves are more intense in hue, with a velvety quality. This aromatic plant is a good mixer; its soft texture combines with silver foliage and contrasts with the harder, shinier leaves of most evergreens. (See Good Companions, left.)

Euonymus japonicus 'Microphyllus Pulchellus' • *Ilex cornuta* • *Pieris japonica* 'Little Heath' • *Rhododendron* 'Patty Bee' •

Ceanothus thyrsiflorus 'Skylark': a fast-growing evergreen with sapphire-blue flowers in early summer.

Flowering shrubs

Evergreen and large deciduous flowering shrubs are the backbone of the garden. They offer the best of both worlds, providing structure, as well as a colourful and sometimes fragrant display. Evergreens are useful for their permanent, year-round qualities, while deciduous shrubs provide seasonally changing interest within the middle layer of the planting picture.

All broad-leaved evergreens flower but those included in previous sections of this book are grown primarily for their foliage. The shrubs described on the following pages are grown for both their leaves and their flowers.

FLOWERING EVERGREENS

Berberis darwinii♡ is often thought of as a hedging plant, but left untrimmed it forms a large shrub, reaching 3m (10ft), with graceful but compact growth and small, shiny dark green, holly-like leaves. In mid-spring the shrub is transformed as the orange-red buds open to tiny vivid orange flowers in clusters all over the branches. It can be pruned or trimmed after flowering to control its size.

The evergreen **California lilacs** (*Ceanothus*) are some of the most popular flowering shrubs. They fulfil the impatient gardener's requirements: fast growth, shiny evergreen leaves and a brilliant display of flowers, even on young plants; most bloom in late spring or early summer, a few in autumn. Ceanothus are not long-lived plants, and eight to ten years is a realistic lifespan; be sure to plant a replacement before a mature specimen expires. They resent pruning, particularly cutting back into old wood, so plant them with sufficient space for their vigorous growth.

Berberis darwinii

EXOTIC FLOWERING SHRUBS *Abutilon vitifolium* var. *album* • *Calycanthus floridus* • *Carpenteria californica* •

***Ceanothus* 'Concha'**♀ is one of the best of the California lilacs, with reddish flower buds and clouds of sapphire blossom in late spring. It has an upright arching habit, so will rise above other shrubs planted in front of it. ***Ceanothus thyrsiflorus* 'Skylark'**♀ is useful for its later flowers in early summer. It has vigorous, upright growth and emerald foliage and bright blue flowers in compact clusters. 'Skylark' is not as spectacular as 'Concha' but is a better mixer; when in flower, there is more green foliage visible between the flowers. It is a good choice for the centre of a large island bed, where it will grow to 3m (10ft).

Choisya ternata♀ is one of the most widely planted shrubs. Forming a rounded bush, up to 1.5m (5ft) high, it has bright green aromatic foliage and clusters of fragrant white flowers in spring and autumn. Choisya grows on any soil but dislikes very wet conditions. It grows in shade but flowers better in sun. The yellow-leaved ***Choisya ternata*** SUNDANCE **('Lich')**♀ (see page 101) is a striking plant but its bright leaves are very dominant in a scheme. ***Choisya* 'Aztec Pearl'**♀ (see also page 127) has much finer foliage and masses of white flowers in late spring. It is an excellent choice for a sheltered site.

Choisya 'Aztec Pearl'

SCENTED EVERGREENS

Mahonia japonica (above) is a tall evergreen with holly-like leaves and sprays of pale yellow, scented flowers, reminiscent of lily-of-the-valley, in winter and early spring. *Osmanthus* × *burkwoodii*♀ (see page 79) and *Pittosporum tobira*♀ (see page 78) produce a worthwhile display of highly fragrant blooms. *Phillyrea angustifolia* (see page 79) has small, creamy-yellow scented flowers in late spring. *Elaeagnus* × *ebbingei* produces very tiny perfumed flowers in autumn. *Choisya ternata*♀ (see page 38) bears fragrant white flowers in spring and again in autumn.

Escallonias are excellent flowering shrubs for well-drained soil. They are a good choice for sunny positions and grow well by the coast; most grow to around 2m (6ft). Not the hardiest of evergreens, they are not plants for cold areas, and even the hardier cultivars may look unhappy after a winter in frosty and exposed gardens. In sheltered situations, ***Escallonia* 'Iveyi'**♀ is one of the finest, with glossy green leaves and large sprays of white flowers throughout summer and autumn. It is a good subject to plant against the house wall, if a large evergreen shrub is required. The pink flowering escallonias are useful evergreens to plant with shrub roses to extend the flowering season. The highly popular ***Escallonia* 'Apple Blossom'**♀, with pink and white flowers, grows to 1m (40in) and is perfect for this purpose. ***Escallonia* 'Peach Blossom'**♀ has peach-pink flowers, and is larger-growing.

Escallonia 'Apple Blossom'

Viburnum tinus needs no introduction. It is a shrub that grows anywhere, even in the dry shade under trees. Its dense habit, evergreen leaves and long flowering period fulfil the ultimate requirements of any gardener. Unfortunately, it has suffered from the effects of over-use in gloomy municipal plantings. However, plant it with lighter, variegated plants, such as *Cornus alba* 'Sibirica Variegata' and *Pittosporum tenuifolium* 'Irene Paterson'♀, and it will be transformed. (See pages 79, 133.)

FLOWERING EVERGREENS FOR ACID SOIL

Those gardening on acid soil will have no shortage of flowering evergreens: rhododendrons (here, 'September Song'), pieris, camellias and evergreen azaleas are the most popular. Those on alkaline soils can grow many of these in pots (see pages 126–29). As well as having evergreen foliage, they are very valuable for a spectacular spring display of flowers.

Crinodendron hookerianum • *Grevillea* 'Robyn Gordon' • *Magnolia liliiflora* 'Nigra' • *Paeonia suffruticosa* •

Hamamelis × intermedia 'Pallida'

Magnolia stellata

Forsythia × intermedia 'Spectabilis'

Syringa vulgaris 'Madame Lemoine'

Philadelphus 'Belle Etoile'

DECIDUOUS FLOWERING SHRUBS

In winter and early spring, many deciduous shrubs flower on bare stems. They have a delicate, fragile quality, without the weight of leaves to accompany the flowers. The **witch hazels** (*Hamamelis*) are some of the earliest to flower. They are magnificent shrubs of open structure that succeed best on fertile, acid or neutral soils. Although many grow large, they are not greedy on space and allow other plants to be grown under them. Many also display superb autumn colour. ***Hamamelis* × *intermedia* 'Pallida'**♀ is one of the most reliable, with pale yellow fragrant flowers that show up well against a dark background. ***Hamamelis* × *intermedia* 'Jelena'**♀ has apricot-orange flowers; in an open position, they are stunning against a blue winter sky.

Many traditional spring-flowering shrubs are large and bulky, so are not plants for key positions in the garden. However, if they can be incorporated with other screening shrubs they contribute a welcome show of colour early in the year. The popularity of ***Forsythia* × *intermedia* 'Spectabilis'** bears testament to this.

Magnolias are among the most exotic flowering shrubs. Their flamboyant blooms grace elegant branches with an air of the Orient. They are spoilt by pruning, so it is important not to choose a variety that is likely to get too large for the situation. ***Magnolia stellata***♀ is the easiest to accommodate, with a more compact habit and smaller flowers that are less prone to weather damage. ***Magnolia stellata* 'Waterlily'**♀, with starry white blooms, is one of the best and most popular cultivars.

The **lilacs** (*Syringa*) are loved for their extravagant sprays of fragrant flowers. They are not the most attractive shrubs in the garden, but the varieties of ***Syringa vulgaris*** are ideal at the back of large borders provided they are hard-pruned annually after flowering. This promotes tall, vigorous stems and flowers at the top of the shrub. ***Syringa vulgaris* 'Madame Lemoine'** bears white flowers opening from cream buds.

In late spring and early summer, no garden should be without the glorious fragrance of a **philadelphus**. For larger

FLOWERING SPECIMEN SHRUBS *Camellia japonica* 'Adolphe Audusson' • *Cercis chinensis* 'Avondale' •

GOOD WITH CLIMBERS

The season of interest of many large deciduous shrubs can be extended by planting light climbers to grow through them.

Try *Philadelphus* 'Belle Etoile'🏆 (1) with *Clematis* 'Alba Luxurians'🏆 (2). The clematis will grow up through the branches of the philadelphus to provide nodding white flowers after those of the philadelphus have faded. Prune the clematis to within 45cm (18in) of the ground in late winter. Cut out some of the branches of the philadelphus immediately after the flowers have faded.

The perennial pea *Lathyrus latifolius* 'Albus'🏆 (3) grows through the ascending branches of *Viburnum plicatum* 'Roseum' (4) to produce pure white blooms after those of the viburnum have faded. The pea dies back to the ground in winter; some of the flowered stems of the viburnum should be cut back after flowering.

Viburnum plicatum f. *tomentosum* 'Mariesii'

Hydrangea paniculata 'Kyushu'

spaces, ***Philadelphus* 'Belle Etoile'**🏆 is a fine choice, with creamy single flowers with maroon blotches and golden stamens in the centres. If some of the shoots that have flowered are cut out after the blooms have faded, the shrub will maintain an elegant, arching habit. (See box, above.) Where space is limited, plant the lovely double-flowering ***Philadelphus* 'Manteau d'Hermine'**🏆, which reaches only 1m (40in) in height.

Viburnums are such a diverse group of plants it is hard to choose the best. ***Viburnum plicatum* f. *tomentosum* 'Mariesii'**🏆, with its horizontal, layered branches, is a magnificent sight in late spring, when the white lacecap flowers are clustered along the branches like a frosted wedding cake. The flowering period is not long, but the shape of the plant is attractive all year. This is a good subject for a rural setting and is large enough to grow as a specimen plant in grass. The snowball bush ***Viburnum plicatum* 'Roseum'** is also suitable for this purpose and is a delight in spring, when the lime-green flowerheads gradually develop into cream then white balls of flowers that hang from the branches. (See box, above.)

Hydrangeas are the stars of the summer and autumn garden. The flowers of the mophead hydrangeas are long-lasting and remain decorative on the plants even after they have faded. ***Hydrangea* 'Preziosa'**🏆 is one of the finest, with purple-tinged foliage and large flowers that open pink and mature to deep red-purple. Both lacecap and mophead hydrangeas grow well in sun or light shade. For the back of the border, ***Hydrangea paniculata*** is an excellent choice if hard-pruned annually in spring. ***Hydrangea paniculata* 'Kyushu'**🏆 is an upright plant, reaching 1.5m (5ft), with syringa-like flowerheads of tiny fertile and larger sterile white florets.

Buddleja 'Lochinch'

Abelia × grandiflora

Lavandula stoechas subsp. *pedunculata*

Philadelphus coronarius 'Variegatus'

DECIDUOUS SHRUBS FOR FOLIAGE AND FLOWERS

In smaller gardens, larger-growing deciduous flowering shrubs that deliver a brief display of flowers and contribute nothing more than green foliage for the rest of the year can be an extravagant use of space. Choose shrubs that provide more enduring foliage interest in addition to the flowers.

Abelia × grandiflora🏆 is a vigorous semi-evergreen shrub with arching branches carrying glossy leaves. The pink flowers are produced from midsummer through autumn and leave the pink calyces on the branches when they fall. Although ultimately large, this shrub can be controlled by cutting some of the branches right back to the base.

The **buddleias** are justly popular for their fragrant summer flowers that are so attractive to bees and butterflies. ***Buddleja* 'Lochinch'**🏆 has fine silver-grey foliage, so is a useful addition to the border from late spring until the leaves fall in autumn. The newer ***Buddleja* 'Silver Anniversary'** has fine silver foliage and white flowers, making it particularly useful for foliage effect in a white planting scheme. (See box, opposite.)

Lavenders are loved for their fragrance and soft hues. However, most are at their peak in midsummer. ***Lavandula stoechas* subsp. *pedunculata***🏆 starts to flower in late spring and with a little deadheading and trimming will continue into autumn. In addition to the winged lavender flowers, the sage-green foliage is wonderfully aromatic and a delightful addition to any planting in full sun on well-drained soil.

There is nothing quite like the fragrance of a **philadelphus** (mock orange), when the beautiful flowers clothe the branches in early summer. ***Philadelphus coronarius* 'Aureus'**🏆 has the added bonus of excellent golden yellow foliage. Although the colour is strong, it works well in yellow schemes and is a good planting partner for euphorbias (see page 101) and *Alchemilla mollis* (see page 106). In shade, the leaves are lime green and in this situation the plant does not run the risk of scorching (which it does in full sun). ***Philadelphus coronarius* 'Variegatus'**🏆 is a pretty shrub, with fragrant white flowers set against a background of soft cream- and green-variegated leaves. It is best grown in semi-shade and is not a good choice for exposed sites.

For those gardening on acid soil, the **deciduous azaleas** are elegant shrubs with an open branch framework that looks good with other plants or on its own. The delicate flowers are reliably produced in late spring, and many possess a wonderful fragrance. After the flowers, there is excellent autumn foliage

OTHER FLOWERING SHRUBS WITH COLOURFUL FOLIAGE *Clerodendrum trichotomum* 'Carnival' •

Rhododendron 'Irene Koster'

GOOD WITH ROSES

Roses are often good planted with other flowering shrubs.

Weigela florida 'Foliis Purpureis'♀ (1) provides early summer flowers against its soft purple-brown leaves. The strong pink flowers of *Rosa* ROSEMOOR ('Austough') (2) follow those of the weigela, and are also shown off against the shrub's dark foliage. Prune the rose in winter, and cut back some of the flowered stems of the weigela once the blooms have faded.

The silver foliage of *Buddleja* 'Silver Anniversary' (3) is a sophisticated partner for the fresh green foliage and the beautiful, pure white blooms of *Rosa* ICEBERG ('Korbin')♀ (4). The white flowers of the buddleia appear as the first flush of roses is fading and before the next appears.

colour to look forward to: a display every bit as worthwhile as the flowers. ***Rhododendron* 'Fireball'**♀, with flame-red blooms, and ***Rhododendron* 'Irene Koster'**♀, with soft pink flowers, are just two varieties that produce fragrant flowers and display good autumn colour. The lovely ***Rhododendron luteum***♀, with yellow, honeysuckle-scented flowers is a must for naturalistic plantings.

Weigelas bear funnel-shaped flowers in summer. Reliable shrubs, they thrive on all soils, including chalk and clay. ***Weigela florida* 'Foliis Purpureis'**♀ has mauve-pink flowers against purple-brown foliage; the leaves are not showy, but it is an excellent mixer and combines well with herbaceous perennials and shrub roses – the early summer flowers of the weigela extend the season of the roses (see box, left). The newer variety ***Weigela florida*** WINE AND ROSES **('Alexandra')** has shinier red-bronze leaves and is a slightly showier alternative. ***Weigela* 'Florida Variegata'**♀ is one of the best variegated shrubs, with the bonus of freely produced pink flowers in early summer. Its loose, arching habit makes it an easy plant to fit into an informal planting scheme.

Cornus mas 'Variegata' • *Fuchsia* 'Genii' • *Hebe* 'Mrs Winder' • *Hebe* 'Silver Queen' • *Hydrangea* 'Preziosa' •

Architectural plants

Plants with strong architectural form have numerous uses in the garden. Their bold shapes become eye-catching focal points in the middle and lower layers of the garden picture, they can be used as individual specimens in pots, in gravel or in ground-cover planting, and they balance the firm presence of stone paving, walls and masonry. In mixed planting, they provide a striking contrast to the soft, rounded forms of many plants.

Although they tend to be associated with contemporary design, the use of architectural plants in gardens is actually nothing new. As early as the 1800s, William Robinson pioneered the inclusion of bold foliage plants and exotics in naturalistic settings.

ARCHITECTURAL EVERGREENS

Fatsia japonica♕ is the ultimate architectural evergreen, with large dark green, shiny lobed leaves. It is a substantial shrub, reaching 2m (6ft) in the open ground, and is an ideal subject for a shady corner. Grown in a pot, it makes a strong statement. When it loses its leaves at the base of the plant and becomes leggy, it can be rejuvenated by hard pruning.

Phormium tenax♕ (New Zealand flax) is a spiky, statuesque evergreen perennial with upright, leathery, fibrous leaves that reach 2m (6ft) in height. It grows to form large clumps and produces even taller, dark red-brown flower stems that resemble wrought iron. The cultivars of phormium with coloured leaves are the most popular in gardens. They are less vigorous than *Phormium tenax* and add colour as well as spiky texture to the planting. ***Phormium* 'Yellow Wave'**♕ is one of the hardiest, with yellow, green-edged leaves that arch at the tips. ***Phormium tenax* 'Atropurpureum'** has upright, pointed leaves in shades of plum and red-brown. ***Phormium* 'Dark Delight'** and ***Phormium* 'Platt's Black'** are smaller-growing varieties, with arching leaves of dark plum-black.

Cordyline australis♕ (New Zealand cabbage palm) has a more severe form than the phormiums and mixes less comfortably with other plants. It is widely used as a centrepiece in seasonal displays, and mature specimens can add exotic effects to more naturalistic schemes. It looks at home in seaside and Mediterranean gardens and is spectacular in flower and heavily scented. In most gardens it is best grown in a pot near to the house, where its architectural form is offset by the solid structure around it. The red forms, such as ***Cordyline australis* 'Torbay Red'**♕, are the most striking and the easiest colour to mix with other plants. The cream-variegated ***Cordyline australis* 'Torbay Dazzler'**♕ is useful with light foliage tones such as ***Griselinia littoralis***♕ (see page 116) and ***Osmanthus heterophyllus* 'Goshiki'** (see page 96).

Chamaerops humilis♕ is one of the hardiest palms, with a dwarf, compact habit and Mediterranean character. Again, it is most at home in a pot or planted into a space in paving or in a gravel or scree setting. ***Chamaerops humilis* 'Vulcano'** has more silver spiky foliage, and the much sought-after ***Chamaerops humilis* var. *argentea*** is pure silver-blue when grown in full sun.

Fatsia japonica

Cordyline australis 'Torbay Red'

Chamaerops humilis var. *argentea*

OTHER SPIKY-LEAVED PLANTS *Agave americana* • *Astelia chathamica* • *Crocosmia* 'Lucifer' • *Iris foetidissima* •

Phormium tenax makes a bold statement with its large, sword-shaped evergreen leaves that soar above the surrounding planting.

Fastigiate (upright-growing) plants are also architectural in character. Larger subjects, for example ***Taxus baccata* 'Fastigiata'**♀, are highly structural when they reach a credible size. Smaller fastigiate plants are used as exclamation marks in the planting. ***Ilex crenata* 'Fastigiata'** is a rigid, upright form of the Japanese holly; its dark green, convex leaves clothe the vertical stems to the base of the plant. (See Good Companions, right.) ***Ligustrum japonicum* 'Rotundifolium'** is an unusual privet with thick, leathery, dark green leaves with wavy, round edges. These are virtually stalkless and cling onto the upright stems to create curious columns. It is dramatic in a contemporary container of marble or steel.

Bold evergreen shrubs, for example ***Viburnum davidii***♀, can have an architectural appearance, depending on how they are planted. If given space and allowed to develop into a regular mound up to 1m (40in) or so high, this shrub is stunning when in good condition. In semi-shade the dark, deeply furrowed leaves are striking and dramatic. (See Good Companions, below.)

GOOD COMPANIONS

Viburnum davidii♀ (1) looks particularly striking partnered with a strongly vertical plant. Bamboos grown for their stems, such as *Phyllostachys aureosulcata* f. *aureocaulis*♀ (2), make excellent companions.

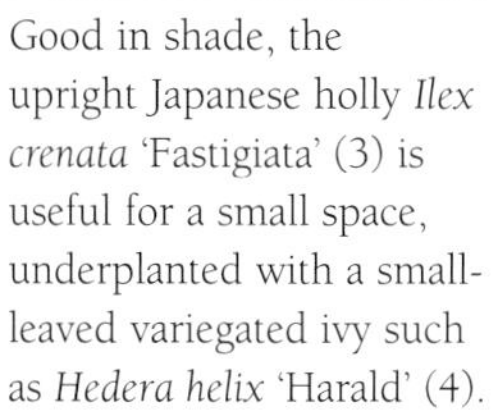

Good in shade, the upright Japanese holly *Ilex crenata* 'Fastigiata' (3) is useful for a small space, underplanted with a small-leaved variegated ivy such as *Hedera helix* 'Harald' (4).

Iris sibirica • *Kniphofia* 'Atlanta' • *Sisyrinchium striatum* • *Stipa gigantea* • *Yucca flaccida* 'Golden Sword' •

Phyllostachys aureosulcata f. *aureocaulis*

Phyllostachys nigra

BAMBOOS FOR ARCHITECTURAL EFFECT

Gardeners have a love-hate relationship with bamboo. There are those who spend their time trying to banish the creeping rhizomes of an invasive species from their garden, and those who cosset and struggle to cultivate the less robust but highly desirable kinds.

Bamboos have many uses: dwarf cultivars make good ground cover in shade; some tall, robust bamboos make excellent shelter plants and screens; those with coloured foliage look striking in containers; but the most handsome are those grown for their stems. They do not like waterlogged soils but enjoy adequate moisture, and are often at their best near water, where their reflection emphasizes their vertical structure.

Among the best bamboos grown for their beautiful stems is ***Phyllostachys nigra***🏆, with its graceful, arching canes that reach 3m (10ft) in height. The stems are green at first, becoming brown and then black when grown in full sun in warmer regions. Another choice bamboo is the hardy ***Phyllostachys aurea***🏆, which forms large clumps of arching canes up to 3m (10ft) high. The canes are green maturing to pale yellow and dull yellow in full sun. ***Phyllostachys aureosulcata* f. *aureocaulis***🏆 (see also page 91) is larger, growing to 5m (15ft), with reddish canes maturing to golden yellow. ***Chusquea culeou***🏆 is a bamboo with a very different profile. The deep green canes form a dense clump. The leaves are more numerous and clothe the canes along their entire length in a bottlebrush effect.

SHOWING OFF BAMBOO STEMS

Bamboos with beautiful stems must be given the opportunity to display them. Their strong, vertical lines should rise unimpeded from gravel or low ground cover. Some of the lower sideshoots can be cleared from the lower part of the plant to display more of the main stems. If planted behind taller shrubs and perennials, they become ordinary tall green shrubs.

USING CONIFERS

Conifers come into their own in the winter and early spring, when their foliage is at its best and they are unchallenged by the green of deciduous shrubs and perennials. In shades of green, gold and brown, their range of colour is only surpassed by their variety of form and texture: upright, spreading, conical, columnar, soft or rigid, there is a conifer great or small to contrast with any other plant form in the garden.

Sometimes the form and foliage of conifers are so different from those of other plants that they do not sit happily alongside them. For example, large golden conifers such as ***Chamaecyparis lawsoniana* 'Stardust'**🏆, with their strong golden colour, conical habit and obviously cultivated look, can look out of place in country gardens. Generally, most conifers look best planted where their individual shape and character can be appreciated, without competition from other plants. They associate well with their own kind, and also with heathers, grasses, phormiums and dwarf hebes. (See also *Taxus baccata*, pages 76–77.)

OTHER PLANTS WITH BOLD FOLIAGE *Bergenia cordifolia* 'Purpurea' • *Canna* TROPICANNA ('Phasion') •

SOME SMALL-GROWING CONIFERS

Conifers are often underrated, but they have many advantages. They are low maintenance, suit contemporary settings as well as more traditional ones, and provide all-year-round interest as they are evergreen. There are many compact conifers for smaller gardens.

Chamaecyparis lawsoniana 'Aurea Densa'♀ (1) has densely packed sprays of golden foliage forming a conical bush, growing slowly to 2m (6ft).

Chamaecyparis obtusa 'Nana Gracilis'♀ has the potential to grow into a large conical shrub but it usually reaches only 2m (6ft). It has emerald-green, shell-like, dense sprays of foliage that are darker in the centre and brighter towards the edges.

Cryptomeria japonica 'Vilmoriniana'♀ is very slow-growing, reaching only 30cm (12in) in 10 years or more. It has dense, crowded foliage forming a globe of dark green that turns reddish purple in winter.

Juniperus communis 'Compressa'♀ forms a dwarf, compact, pointed column of silver green slowly reaching 60cm (2ft); it is a good subject for a pot. (See page 125.)

Picea pungens 'Globosa'♀ is a compact form of the blue spruce, growing into a flattened, broad globe of dense, steel-blue foliage; it reaches 60cm (2ft) in height.

Thuja occidentalis 'Smaragd'♀ (2) is particularly noteworthy as a structural, architectural plant. It grows to form a narrow cone, up to 3m (10ft) high, of tightly packed bright green foliage. It is a useful alternative to clipped box cones and suits formal settings as well as bringing structure and height to mixed plantings.

1

2

TRIMMED AND TRAINED PLANTS FOR ARCHITECTURAL EFFECT

Shaped plants are commonly used as specimens in formal settings but they are also valuable exclamation marks in more informal schemes. *Buxus sempervirens*♀ (common box) is one of the easiest to accommodate and is very useful trimmed into balls and cones (see page 77). *Laurus nobilis*♀ (sweet bay) is one of the most widely used, particularly as a standard (see page 76). *Taxus baccata*♀ (yew), with its dense, bushy habit, is the most architectural of all hedging plants, and is also useful for topiary (right, see also pages 76–77). *Ligustrum delavayanum*, a privet with small, dark green leaves, is a useful, faster-growing alternative to box.

GOOD COMPANIONS

(1) The silver-green, jigsaw-shaped leaves of *Macleaya microcarpa* stand out dramatically against the round, plum-purple foliage of *Cotinus coggygria* 'Royal Purple'♀.

(2) The deep, violet-blue flowers of *Aconitum* 'Spark's Variety'♀ are the perfect partners for the architectural flower spikes of *Acanthus* 'Summer Beauty'.

ARCHITECTURAL PERENNIALS

Many herbaceous perennials have wonderfully architectural leaves of large and highly dramatic proportions. Those gardening on wet soil will find no shortage of bold foliage effects among the **rodgersias**, **ligularias**, **darmera** and **rheums**, for example the vast-leaved ***Rheum palmatum***. However, the most dramatic of all perennials must be the massive ***Gunnera manicata***♀, with its huge rhubarb-like foliage that towers overhead in summer.

In drier conditions, the evergreen, woody-based **euphorbias** are useful. ***Euphorbia mellifera***♀ (honey spurge) forms a large bush up to 2m (6ft) high, with upright stems carrying softly pointed, light green leaves. Reddish flower clusters appear at the top of the branches in late spring and early summer. It is an impressive plant to grow against a sunny wall, where it will revel in the warm, dry conditions.

Acanthus spinosus♀, with its large, spiny green leaves and statuesque flower spikes, has great presence in the border or as a specimen plant rising from gravel or alongside paving. It grows in sun or partial shade on most soils.

Hostas have a great architectural quality and beautiful leaf shapes. The large-leaved hostas are especially dramatic, particularly ***Hosta* 'Sum and Substance'**♀, with its enormous broad, yellow-green leaves. ***Hosta sieboldiana* var. *elegans***♀ has large, veined and puckered blue-green leaves and looks particularly good when planted with ***Euphorbia griffithii* 'Fireglow'**.

Macleaya cordata♀ and ***Macleaya microcarpa*** are ideal spreading through the back of the border between shrubs, which lend support to their 2.5m (8ft) stems. The flowers are secondary to their intriguing leaves. (See Good Companions, left.) They can be invasive.

OTHER PERENNIALS WITH A VERTICAL HABIT *Aconitum* 'Stainless Steel' • *Campanula latiloba* •

ARCHITECTURAL FLOWERHEADS

Lupins bear beautiful spikes in early summer. Most varieties are about 90cm (3ft) tall. (1) *Lupinus polyphyllus* hybrid.

Foxtail lilies have spectacular bottlebrush spikes in summer. Some varieties reach over 2m (6ft) high. (2) *Eremurus* × *isabellinus* 'Cleopatra'.

Foxgloves bear tiny tubular flowers on spikes up to 2m (6ft) high in midsummer. (3) *Digitalis ferruginea*♀.

Delphiniums have glorious spikes in shades of blue, purple, pink, and white in summer; some varieties reach over 2m (6ft). (4) *Delphinium elatum* group.

The euphorbias include *Euphorbia characias* (5): its upright stems are clothed in blue-green leaves and topped with showy, lime-green flowerheads in spring.

Red hot pokers have eye-catching spikes of orange, red or yellow flowers from early summer to autumn. (6) *Kniphofia* 'Royal Standard'♀.

1  2  3  4  5  6

Euphorbia griffithii 'Fireglow'

Hosta sieboldiana var. *elegans*

Ligularia 'The Rocket' • *Salvia* × *superba* • *Verbascum chaixii* 'Album' • *Veronicastrum virginicum* •

Colourful foliage

Variety in the colour and texture of foliage is the essence of good planting. Leaves last longer than flowers so will carry, or accentuate, any colour theme. Evergreens with colourful foliage lighten the green canopy of summer and add colour and interest to the winter garden.

VARIEGATED FOLIAGE

Variegated leaves add variety to the heavy green of midsummer foliage and provide colour, usually gold or white, creating the same effect as adding a plant with flowers of these colours. In winter, variegated evergreens stand out against bare branches and winter stems. If used in moderation, variegated plants have a place in most gardens, but they are a phenomenon of cultivated gardens and are therefore normally out of place in naturalistic planting schemes.

There are relatively few good trees with variegated foliage. However, they are useful to add light colour above eye level. In a small garden, a variegated tree such as ***Acer negundo*** **'Elegans'** can be positioned effectively to break up the dark wall of a neighbouring house. In a large garden, the cream and green ***Acer platanoides*** **'Drummondii'** will stand out beautifully against surrounding trees with darker foliage. In both cases, shoots that have 'reverted' (plain green shoots) must be removed as they appear, or they will eventually predominate.

Acer platanoides 'Drummondii'

Elaeagnus pungens 'Frederici'

Osmanthus heterophyllus 'Goshiki'

Cornus controversa **'Variegata'**♀ can be grown as a specimen shrub or a small tree. In the longer term, it will reach 5m (15ft) or more and is a beautiful plant at every stage of its life. Horizontal layered branches carry creamy, white-edged, pale green leaves. It is a lovely 'see-through' plant, so is wonderful when planted in the foreground; it is at its best in green and white planting schemes. In smaller spaces, choose ***Cornus alternifolia*** **'Argentea'**♀, which has smaller, white-variegated leaves and a similar, if lighter habit. It can be grown to give the effect of a small tree with layered branches by thinning the stems to one or two shoots at an early age.

Evergreen shrubs offer the gardener the greatest choice of variegation. Variegated forms of **elaeagnus** are widely planted for their evergreen foliage and their bulky form. ***Elaeagnus pungens*** **'Frederici'** has soft yellow leaves narrowly edged with green, and is more subtle and slow-growing than the popular ***Elaeagnus pungens*** **'Maculata'**. ***Elaeagnus pungens*** **'Hosuba-fukurin'** is another compact plant, with green leaves edged with yellow.

Osmanthus are holly-like, evergreen shrubs with a more rounded, compact habit than elaeagnus. ***Osmanthus heterophyllus*** **'Variegatus'**♀ has dark green leaves edged with white, and is superb for shade. (See Good Companions, page 135.) The most popular cultivar is ***Osmanthus heterophyllus*** **'Goshiki'**, which has spiny leaves streaked cream,

USING VARIEGATIONS

Variegated plants with the same constituent colours can be combined to great effect to add impact to planting schemes, particularly in the presence of plain green foliage. Bold white and green variegations, such as *Hosta* 'Patriot' (1), work with more subtle, finer white and green variegations as in *Brunnera macrophylla* 'Jack Frost' (2).

Different degrees of yellow variegation can be combined in a similar way. However, white and yellow variegations do not mix happily. Yellow-variegated plants, like *Hosta* 'June' (3), appear stronger and brighter when combined with golden foliage plants such as *Sambucus racemosa* 'Sutherland Gold'🏆 (4), while plain yellow leaves detract from the subtlety of white and green variegations.

copper and dark green. It forms a compact, rounded shrub up to 1m (40in) or more high, and combines well with a wide variety of other plants.

Pittosporums are relatively quick-growing evergreen shrubs that add light height to the back of a border. The ever-popular ***Pittosporum* 'Garnettii'**🏆 has grey-green leaves edged with white, giving a silver effect that will lift any mixed planting of pastel shades. (See Good Companions, page 99.) The slower-growing and shorter ***Pittosporum tenuifolium* 'Irene Paterson'**🏆 is brighter, with peridot-green foliage suffused with cream. The new growth is creamy-white and is particularly striking.

Of the deciduous variegated shrubs, **dogwoods** (*Cornus*) reign supreme. There are a number of varieties of *Cornus alba* with either gold or white variegations. ***Cornus alba* 'Elegantissima'**🏆 is the best known of the white-variegated kinds. However, it grows into a large shrub if not cut back regularly. ***Cornus alba* 'Sibirica Variegata'** is smaller, with pink-tinged, white-variegated leaves; it is more suitable for smaller spaces. ***Cornus alba* IVORY HALO ('Bailhalo')** is another compact selection, with cream-edged leaves and red stems in winter. ***Cornus alba* 'Gouchaultii'** and ***Cornus alba* 'Spaethii'**🏆 are similar, both with pretty gold-variegated foliage. (See Good Companions, page 101.) The former has a pink tinge and is a more subtle shade of gold, making it easier to mix with other plants. ***Cornus mas* 'Variegata'**🏆 is one of the finest variegated shrubs, with oval, pointed leaves, dark green in the centre, with a broad cream margin. It has an open habit, and the straight bare twigs are covered with yellow flower clusters in early spring. These are followed by red, cherry-like fruits in late summer.

Variegated hostas, such as the striking ***Hosta* 'Patriot'**, with its bold, white-margined leaves, will lighten any shady corner and provide a focal point in ground-cover plantings of periwinkle (*Vinca*) and pachysandra. A yellow-variegated hosta, such as the lovely ***Hosta* 'June' (Tardiana Group)**, can be underplanted with the lesser periwinkle ***Vinca minor* 'Illumination'**, which has dark green, gold-streaked leaves. The periwinkle will provide evergreen ground cover when the hosta dies down. (See Good Companions, page 81.)

***Brunnera macrophylla* 'Jack Frost'** is a delightful plant for semi-shade. It has bright blue, forget-me-not flowers in early spring. The semi-evergreen leaves are heart-shaped and etched with silver.

Pittosporum tenuifolium 'Irene Paterson'

Cornus mas 'Variegata'

Prunus cerasifera 'Nigra'

Acer palmatum 'Bloodgood'

Cotinus coggygria 'Royal Purple'

Acer palmatum var. *dissectum* 'Crimson Queen'

PLANT PURPLE IN SUN

Purple-leaved shrubs and perennials need good light, including some direct sunlight, to develop their best leaf colour. In shade, purple foliage loses its intensity and becomes greenish brown in colour.

PLUM AND PURPLE LEAVES

Purple and plum foliage is a good mixer, as its dark, rich tones combine easily with other colours. It strengthens softer colours such as pink, lilac and pale blue, providing a deep contrast, and offers a dramatic background for bold, bright colours, enhancing their strength. Plum and purple leaves also combine well with soft silver foliage; the partnership is even more striking in the presence of white flowers.

Trees with purple leaves make a bold statement above the rest of the garden picture. The purple-leaved plum ***Prunus cerasifera*** **'Nigra'**🏆 produces small, deep purple leaves. Its billowing, rounded form has bold presence without weight, and its light branches have plenty of texture and movement. (See also page 151.) In larger gardens, ***Acer platanoides*** **'Crimson King'**🏆 and ***Fagus sylvatica*** **'Riversii'**🏆 are an excellent choice. (See page 141.)

The **Japanese maples** are normally grown as shrubs but fulfil the role of small trees in pots and small spaces. The red- and purple-leaved varieties are some of the most beautiful coloured-foliage shrubs. Their soft, layered branches stir in the slightest breeze, and their foliage is entrancing from the time the fresh leaves emerge until they turn rich shades in autumn. Red-leaved maples will grow in full sun, but they need adequate moisture at the roots and protection from strong winds. ***Acer palmatum*** **'Bloodgood'**🏆 is widely planted and one of the best cultivars. It is a strong plant, with red-purple foliage that is retained well into autumn. Varieties of the Dissectum group (*Acer palmatum* var. *dissectum*🏆) usually have a more rounded, lower-growing habit than the straight *Acer palmatum* cultivars. ***Acer palmatum*** **var.** ***dissectum*** **'Crimson Queen'**🏆 is one of the finest Dissectum group acers, with finely cut purple foliage.

The **smoke bushes** (*Cotinus*) have rounded leaves and clouds of tiny flowers in late summer. There are several purple-leaved varieties, with dark, satin-like foliage with great depth of colour. They are late to come into leaf, rarely showing any growth before late spring, but they do display wonderful autumn colour. ***Cotinus*** **'Grace'** is a vigorous, upright shrub with light, copper-purple foliage turning flame-red in autumn. Plant it where the late afternoon sun will shine through the leaves for dramatic effect. ***Cotinus coggygria*** **'Royal Purple'**🏆 has smaller, deep wine-purple foliage. It is one of the most popular varieties and forms a superb large, rounded background shrub up to 3m (10ft) tall. (See page 94 and Good Companions, opposite.)

Physocarpus opulifolius **'Diabolo'**🏆 is one of the most useful of all the dark-leaved deciduous shrubs. It is upright in habit, and selective hard-pruning will keep it narrow and upright. The leaves are dark purple-black and maple-like. It is an ideal subject to plant with bold, late-flowering perennials such as heleniums and rudbeckias or pittosporums. It also looks good with euonymus. (See Good Companions, opposite.)

OTHER GOOD PLUM- AND PURPLE-LEAVED SHRUBS *Berberis thunbergii* f. *atropurpurea* 'Helmond Pillar' •

Sambucus nigra f. *porphyrophylla* 'Eva'

Bergenia purpurascens

Heuchera 'Plum Pudding'

The purple **elders** are vigorous plants that respond well to hard-pruning in early spring. This results in vigorous upright branches and good foliage colour. ***Sambucus nigra*** **f.** ***porphyrophylla*** **'Eva'** ('Black Lace') has finely divided, intense purple-black leaves. Its light structure combines well with white-variegated shrubs. (See page 127.)

There are few purple-leaved evergreen shrubs but one of the most worthwhile for gardens is ***Pittosporum tenuifolium*** **'Tom Thumb'**🏆. This is one of the most dramatic shrubs in the garden in winter, when it forms a low-growing, dense, almost black cone of foliage.

Some of the purple **hebes** are useful in milder areas. ***Hebe*** **'Mrs Winder'**🏆 is an old variety but still one of the best, with blue flowers and small, shiny, purple-brown leaves. ***Hebe*** **'Pascal'**🏆 and ***Hebe*** **'Caledonia'**🏆 both have red-tinged foliage in winter but are green in the summer months.

When it comes to perennials, the deep burgundy foliage of ***Lysimachia ciliata*** **'Firecracker'**🏆 is a garden essential; the small yellow flowers in midsummer are of secondary importance. The upright stems emerge in late spring, and are dark burgundy with similarly coloured leaves. Cut them back in midsummer, as they regrow to maintain their foliage quality rather than producing flowers. (See Good Companions, left.)

Bergenias that provide foliage colour in winter combine superbly with the bare, colourful stems of *Cornus alba* and *Cornus sanguinea* varieties. The round, shiny leaves of the bergenias are a total contrast to the stark, upright wands of the cornus. ***Bergenia purpurascens***🏆 and ***Bergenia cordifolia*** **'Purpurea'**🏆 both adopt mahogany-purple hues in winter and early spring.

Purple-leaved **heucheras** are some of the best mixers in the garden, succeeding on most soils in sun or shade. By adding depth to the lower layer of planting, they lift lighter subjects. They are evergreen, so they add winter interest and can be used as planting companions for hybrid hellebores. ***Heuchera*** **'Plum Pudding'** is one of the most popular; it has a loose habit and large, plum-coloured leaves. Reaching 30cm (12in) in height, it will not be lost in the border. (See Good Companions, page 83.)

GOOD COMPANIONS

Cotinus coggygria 'Royal Purple'🏆 (1) and *Euonymus fortunei* 'Silver Queen' (2): the latter's shiny cream- and green-variegated leaves provide interest in winter, after the leaves of the smoke bush have fallen.

The dark, black-purple leaves of *Physocarpus opulifolius* 'Diabolo'🏆 (3) contrast with the silver-green of *Pittosporum* 'Garnettii'🏆 (4). The latter is evergreen, providing foliage interest in winter.

The leaves of *Lysimachia ciliata* 'Firecracker'🏆 (5) are dramatic with the early lime-yellow foliage of *Philadelphus coronarius* 'Aureus'🏆 and the vivid lime flowers of *Euphorbia cyparissias* 'Fens Ruby' (6).

Cercis canadensis 'Forest Pansy' • *Pittosporum tenuifolium* 'Purpureum' • *Salvia officinalis* 'Purpurascens' •

Robinia pseudoacacia 'Frisia'

Gleditsia triacanthos 'Sunburst'

Choisya GOLDFINGERS

GOLDEN FOLIAGE

Gold-leaved plants are uplifting: they add a ray of sunshine to a planting scheme and will brighten the dullest corner. Golden foliage mixes well with golden variegations and with yellow, orange and blue flowers. It makes a fresh partner for white but clashes with pink. Used wisely in the garden, gold can bring a planting to life; if positioned carelessly, it can overpower and destroy the effect of other plants.

***Robinia pseudoacacia* 'Frisia'**♀ is the most popular golden tree. Graceful branches are weighed down with abundant soft yellow foliage throughout summer, the colour becoming richer and more intense as summer moves into autumn. It is a substantial tree when mature, reaching 15m (50ft), and looks very effective with large purple foliage shrubs, such as *Cotinus coggygria* 'Royal Purple'♀ (see Good Companions, page 99). Robinias are not good for exposed sites, as they have brittle branches that snap easily. ***Gleditsia triacanthos* 'Sunburst'**♀ creates a similar effect, but with more horizontal, stiffer branches and smaller leaves it is better for windy sites.

***Choisya ternata* SUNDANCE ('Lich')**♀ is the most popular golden evergreen shrub, with white flowers in spring and more again in autumn. A rounded, dome-shaped bush, it is an incredibly strong colour when grown in full sun but a more subtle lime green in shade. It is definitely a plant to partner with gold variegations, which will dilute and spread its effect. (See Good Companions, opposite.) The narrower-leaved ***Choisya* GOLDFINGERS ('Limo')** is a softer colour, but it is less robust, takes time to establish and bleaches in full sun.

***Lonicera nitida* 'Baggesen's Gold'**♀ is a more useful yellow foliage evergreen with tiny, yellow-green leaves crowded on fine stems. It can be pruned to create a

POSITIONING GOLDEN FOLIAGE SHRUBS

Yellow attracts the eye, so always plant golden yellow foliage shrubs where you want to draw attention, never where you want to conceal something. In a mixed scheme, yellow foliage will always be a dominant feature, so distribute it throughout the planting to dilute the effect. Some yellow foliage plants scorch in sun but all lose the intensity of their colour in shade.

OTHER GOOD GOLDEN SHRUBS *Erica carnea* 'Aurea' • *Fuchsia* 'Genii' • *Physocarpus opulifolius* 'Dart's Gold' •

Philadelphus coronarius 'Aureus'

denser effect or left to grow freely, when it will produce soft, arching sprays of foliage. The colour is soft enough to mix in most colour schemes.

Cotinus GOLDEN SPIRIT

The deciduous golden foliage shrubs are easier to use than evergreens, because their foliage colour is prevalent only when there is plenty of other colour in the garden. ***Philadelphus coronarius* 'Aureus'**🏆 is a light, fairly upright shrub with fragrant white flowers in early summer as well as bright golden foliage.

GOOD COMPANIONS

The form and foliage colour of the evergreen *Euphorbia characias* subsp. *wulfenii* 'Lambrook Gold'🏆 (1) contrast well with the woody stems and yellow leaves of *Philadelphus coronarius* 'Aureus'🏆 (2).

The bold, bright yellow variegation of *Euonymus japonicus* 'Chollipo'🏆 (3) is diluted and softened by the smaller leaves and more subtle colouring of *Lonicera nitida* 'Baggesen's Gold'🏆 (4).

The soft colouring of *Cornus alba* 'Spaethii'🏆 (5) dilutes the brash, bright yellow of *Choisya ternata* SUNDANCE ('Lich')🏆 (6). In winter the red cornus stems are shown off against the choisya's evergreen leaves.

Cornus alba 'Aurea'

The leaves are a sharp greenish-yellow when they emerge in spring, becoming bright golden yellow throughout summer. In a shady position they become lime-green. This is a resilient plant that does not scorch badly in full sun. (See Good Companions, left.)

***Cotinus* GOLDEN SPIRIT ('Ancot')** also grows in sun or shade, and has rounded, golden yellow leaves, colouring to flame in autumn. While the plant is in leaf, it is superb if positioned where light will shine through the leaves. ***Cornus alba* 'Aurea'**🏆 is a faster-growing alternative, with upright red stems that are revealed when the leaves fall in winter. Hard-prune the plant in early spring to promote bright, vigorous stems. (See Good Companions, page 79.)

***Sambucus racemosa* 'Sutherland Gold'**🏆 has finely cut leaves that are copper at the branch tips and golden yellow when mature. It is a vigorous shrub and, like all elders, it benefits from hard-pruning of some of the stems in late winter. Its informal habit makes it a good mixer with other woody plants, and it is particularly useful in informal and rural gardens. (See page 97.)

Rubus cockburnianus 'Goldenvale' • *Spiraea japonica* 'Candlelight' • *Weigela* BRIANT RUBIDOR ('Olympiade') •

Pyrus salicifolia 'Pendula'

Elaeagnus 'Quicksilver'

SILVER-LEAVED PLANTS

Most silver foliage plants hail from Mediterranean climates, so they enjoy well-drained soil and full sun and they tolerate drought. Silver foliage is mostly found in the lower layer of planting, because the natural habitat of many silver foliage shrubs is dry scrubland and plants stay small to avoid desiccation. Many silver subjects are aromatic, adding another quality to the planting. Silver foliage reflects light. It stands out boldly against green and plum foliage and is also soft and flattering, enhancing pink and lilac, and being the perfect partner for blue and white.

Trees with silver foliage are wonderfully light and ethereal. They look good against a dark background, as well as other trees or the brickwork of a house. ***Sorbus aria* 'Lutescens'**🏆 is a round-headed tree with stiffly curved dark stems. The unfurling silver-grey leaves are unmissable in spring and reward again with rich yellow autumn colour. For much of the year, the leaves are a pale sage-green with a silver-green reverse. ***Pyrus salicifolia* 'Pendula'**🏆 is a small, weeping tree with grey, willow-like leaves and clusters of creamy-white flowers in spring. It has an awkward, angular habit when young, but soon develops a beautiful broad, weeping habit. Careful pruning will keep it in shape and allow planting beneath the branches. It is a good host for a honeysuckle or light-growing clematis.

The olive, ***Olea europaea***, is becoming increasingly popular. It has beautiful evergreen silver foliage and grey stems. Grown as a small standard, it is ideal for a courtyard, perhaps in a large container. It can be trimmed and trained, but if left to grow naturally it has a graceful habit and is perfect in a Mediterranean scheme.

Elaeagnus* × *ebbingei is a large, fast-growing evergreen shrub with silver-backed leaves. It makes an excellent screening shrub and is resistant to maritime exposure. ***Elaeagnus* 'Quicksilver'**🏆 is perhaps the most striking large silver shrub. Arching branches carry narrow, silver, deciduous leaves and tiny fragrant flowers in summer. With a broad, spreading habit and a height of 4m (12ft) or more, it is ideal at the back of a border, perhaps behind perennials or shrub roses. Some **buddleias** also have silver-grey foliage: ***Buddleja* 'Lochinch'**🏆 (see page 88) and **'Silver Anniversary'** (see page 89) are two of the best.

Ozothamnus rosmarinifolius* 'Silver Jubilee'**🏆 is an upright evergreen shrub with stout stems clothed in tiny, pointed silver leaves, not unlike those of a heather or conifer. Reaching 1m (40in) or more, it is useful to provide height behind lavenders or other low silver shrubs. ***Olearia stellulata (*Olearia* × *scilloniensis*) has small, leathery leaves with a silver-white reverse. Upright branches arch under the weight of white daisy flowers in late spring.

***Brachyglottis* (Dunedin Group) 'Sunshine'** is one of the most versatile silver-grey shrubs, more tolerant of wet weather and damp soil than others. If pruned regularly to remove the gaudy

Ozothamnus rosmarinifolius 'Silver Jubilee'

OTHER GOOD SILVER SHRUBS *Hebe pinguifolia* 'Pagei' • *Lotus hirsutus* • *Perovskia* 'Blue Spire' •

yellow flowers, it maintains a compact habit and is a good mixer in the border.

Dwarf silver shrubs suit borders alongside paths and paved areas where they soften the stone. They also enjoy the dry conditions when planted in gravel and in pots. They are useful at the front of a border filled with roses and perennials, where they provide light structure in the foreground and cover the lower stems and branches of subjects behind them.

Convolvulus cneorum♀ is perhaps the most silver shrub of all, with narrow, silky silver leaves and white trumpet flowers. It reaches around 60 x 60cm (2 x 2ft). The finely cut, felty foliage of ***Santolina chamaecyparissus***♀ is at its best if the plant is trimmed in spring and again when in flower in summer. Cut back to where new growth is emerging half way down the branches. Santolina makes an excellent dwarf hedge. (See also page 121.)

GOOD COMPANIONS

The silver foliage of *Helichrysum italicum* subsp. *serotinum* conceals the fading foliage of *Allium* 'Globemaster'♀, while providing the perfect background for its starry silver-lilac flowers.

Helianthemum 'Cerise Queen'♀ (1) enjoys the same sunny, dry conditions as *Lavandula angustifolia* 'Hidcote'♀ (2). The lavender blooms later than the sun rose, extending the flowering season.

Plant *Artemisia ludoviciana* 'Valerie Finnis'♀ (3) at the front of a border to rise above *Geranium* 'Johnson's Blue'♀ (4), or to create silver threads weaving among the sapphire spikes of *Salvia* × *superba*♀.

Helichrysum italicum♀ has spiky, silver aromatic foliage. It retains its silver colour throughout the winter and is more tolerant of damp than most silver shrubs. (See Good Companions, left.)

The **lavenders** are perhaps the most widely planted dwarf shrubs. Silver aromatic foliage and blue fragrant flowers characterize the plant, although there are many variations. ***Lavandula angustifolia* 'Hidcote'**♀ is one of the most popular, with a compact habit, silver-green leaves and deep blue flowers. Trim the plant after flowering to encourage new silver growth that will retain its colour through winter. (See Good Companions, left.) There are many varieties of lavender; as a rule of thumb, the cultivars with narrow leaves and compact flowerheads are the hardiest.

One of the finest perennials with silver leaves is ***Artemisia ludoviciana* 'Valerie Finnis'**♀. Upright stems grow to 60cm (2ft) or more from creeping underground stems; the coarsely serrated leaves provide soft, light grey highlights in the border. (See Good Companions, left.)

Gertrude Jekyll was very fond of ***Stachys byzantina***, using the silver-grey, felted leaves to soften the edges of a path or beds in a terrace. It should be cut back before or during flowering. ***Stachys byzantina* 'Silver Carpet'** produces few flowers and maintains its foliage quality. As underplanting with shrubs in sun or semi-shade, it both covers the ground and reflects light into the plants above it.

Potentilla fruticosa 'Manchu' • *Rosa glauca* • *Salix elaeagnus* subsp. *angustifolia* • *Teucrium fruticans* •

Adding colour with flowers

While trees and shrubs provide permanent structure and long-lasting foliage interest, you can introduce exciting seasonal colour and variety using perennials, annuals, biennials, bulbs and climbers. There are beautiful flowers for all seasons, including winter, when containers and beds near the house can be filled with bedding subjects to bring a splash of vibrant colour and cheer to the garden at an otherwise quiet and sparse time of the year.

The perennials *Astrantia* 'Hadspen Blood' and *Penstemon* 'Andenken an Friedrich Hahn' add glorious, rich ruby tones to this summer border.

Perennials with a long flowering period, or those with shapes that differ considerably from existing plants, are particularly good choices to add to the border. These include some of our most popular border plants, their wide use being a testimony to their ability to fit into most gardens.

Achilleas are useful not only for their light, feathery foliage but also for their long-lasting flowers, which are produced over a long period throughout summer. Those with large, flattened flowerheads, such as ***Achillea* 'Moonshine'**♀ and ***Achillea filipendulina* 'Gold Plate'**♀, have a striking flower form that is dramatic without being heavy. Instead of cutting them back after flowering, leave the faded flowerheads for winter interest in the border: they are beautiful when dried, and exquisite when etched with frost. The cultivars of ***Achillea millefolium*** include some very attractive colours that are good mixers, particularly the rich cherry ***Achillea* 'Summerwine'**♀ and ***Achillea* 'Terracotta'**.

Astrantias fit into any scheme in sun or semi-shade. Their attractive, star-shaped flowers are long-lasting and are

Achillea 'Terracotta'

carried on upright stems reaching around 60cm (2ft), well above the foliage. Astrantias are light, pretty plants that mix well with herbaceous geraniums and hostas. They flower for a long season and will re-bloom reliably if cut back after the first flush of flowers. ***Astrantia major*** is white, tinged green, and is the best mixer. ***Astrantia maxima*** is soft pink, and the lovely ***Astrantia* 'Hadspen Blood'** is dark red; the latter mixes well with red foliage shrubs and heucheras.

Aquilegias and **polemoniums** are useful for early colour and variety. In both cases, the flowers are carried on tall stems above the foliage, so they float above the low, developing foliage of later-flowering perennials. On light soils, both will seed freely so they are good plants to drift through existing planting and hold a scheme together. ***Aquilegia vulgaris*** may be violet, blue, pink or white. (See page 140.)

Crocosmias are valued for their bright orange, yellow or red flowers that liven up a sunny border in late summer and early autumn. However, the sharp form of their sword-shaped leaves contributes variety and texture for much longer. ***Crocosmia* 'Lucifer'**♀ is perhaps the tallest and most impressive, with broad, sword-shaped foliage and vivid scarlet flowers on tall stems reaching 1m (40in); it is a subject for farther back in the border.

Aquilegia vulgaris

Crocosmia 'Lucifer'

Helleborus* × *hybridus varieties add interest in winter and early spring. These wonderful plants have many uses in the garden, but chiefly they transform the dull void left by other herbaceous perennials in the winter. If planted between daylilies (*Hemerocallis*), which flower mainly between late spring and late summer, or under shrubs at the back of a border, they can have their weeks of glory without competition and can then enjoy the shade of their neighbours when they are at their least beautiful in the summer months.

Penstemon hybrids, with their shrubby habit and evergreen foliage, flower from early summer through to early winter. They carry spikes of tubular, bell-shaped flowers in a range of colours from white, through pink to red and deepest purple. Penstemons flower best in sun but will grow in semi-shade in virtually any soil apart from very wet conditions. They combine well with shrub roses and perennials that have a short, early season, for example poppies and peonies.

In dry, sunny situations ***Sisyrinchium striatum*** adds spikes to the front of a border with its 60cm (2ft) high stems of small cream flowers in midsummer. It transforms clumps of nepeta and alchemilla and works well with lavenders and helianthemums.

LIFTING THE PLANTING

Perennials that produce light flower spikes are ideal to combine with those that grow as soft mounds of foliage. *Digitalis lutea*, *Linaria purpurea* and *Sisyrinchium striatum* (right) are all ideal plants to drift among other plants at the front of a border. Grasses that produce tall flower stems, such *Stipa gigantea*♀, *Miscanthus* 'Yakushima Dwarf' and *Panicum virgatum*, can be used in a similar way, as 'see-through' plants that will increase the perspective and depth of the planting.

Helleborus × *hybridus*

Alchemilla mollis

Euphorbia characias subsp. *wulfenii* 'Lambrook Gold'

Salvia viridis var. *comata*

Alchemilla mollis♀ is a versatile plant with fresh-looking, soft green leaves and stems of frothy, lime-green flowers. Those with bare soil in sun or shade should add it without hesitation: it will seed and colonize, creating a blanket of soft green, and it is the perfect mixer with any other colour. Use it as an edging plant to fill the space under roses, and plant it to spill into gravel; it is also ideal for softening the edges of steps or paving. Some gardeners dislike its invasive tendencies, while others praise its resilience and versatility.

The larger **euphorbias**, such as ***Euphorbia characias*** **subsp.** ***wulfenii*** **'Lambrook Gold'**♀, are fast-growing alternatives to shrubs. With lime-green flowers in spring and a rounded form, they quickly fill a gap on well-drained soil in sun or semi-shade. (See also Good Companions, page 101.) The white-variegated ***Euphorbia*** SILVER SWAN **('Wilcott')** is a must to add to any garden with the right growing conditions. It is striking in form and colour, and makes an excellent focal point against evergreens or silver-variegated shrubs.

HARDY ANNUALS AND BIENNIALS

Some hardy annuals and biennials – those that are not killed by a few degrees of frost – will self-seed on light soils, making themselves a permanent feature in the border. These are useful to introduce colourful informality into a garden, and when trying to rejuvenate existing planting they are very useful gap-fillers. In subsequent years, the number and distribution of plants can be controlled by weeding and replanting. Some are exceptionally successful at settling themselves in among existing planting. They mix well with herbaceous perennials, and look more natural in the herbaceous border than colourful exotics.

Nigella damascena (love-in-a-mist) is a pretty, delicate plant, with starry

ANNUALS AND BIENNIALS

An annual grows from seed and flowers, sets seed and dies all in one growing season. A biennial grows and makes a rosette of leaves in the first year, and the following season it flowers, sets seed and dies. If a display of flowers is required every year from a biennial, then seed will need to be sown in consecutive years initially. Examples of biennials include honesty (*Lunaria annua*) and foxglove (*Digitalis purpurea*, below).

PLANTS FOR WINTER COLOUR *Cyclamen mirabile* • *Erica carnea* • *Euonymus fortunei* 'Emerald 'n' Gold' •

Nigella 'Miss Jekyll'

Briza maxima

flowers in a haze of finely cut foliage. The heavenly blue ***Nigella* 'Miss Jekyll'** is the best mixer and will combine in any colour scheme.

Salvia viridis* var. *comata (clary sage) is an aromatic plant with soft, sage-green foliage and spikes of coloured bracts that last well into autumn. Colours include white, bright pink and deep blue; it is particularly useful among shrub roses and to fill gaps between newly planted perennials, such as delphiniums and lupins. It will also prolong the season.

Lunaria annua (honesty) is useful to brighten up dull spots in poor soil along the base of a hedge or at the base of a wall or under established shrubs. A biennial, it bears bright, magenta-purple

Lunaria annua

flowers in the second year, followed by the familiar papery, silver seedheads. There are pink and white forms.

Briza maxima (quaking grass) mixes well with perennials and other grasses. Its delicate stems and dainty, moving flowerheads may not be the showiest subjects in a border, but it adds lightness as well as movement and, if distributed throughout the planting, it helps to pull a scheme together.

HALF-HARDY ANNUALS

Most bedding plants are not frost hardy, so they are introduced into the garden in late spring, after danger of frost has passed. Many plants used in this way are perennial in their native environment but are treated as annuals in cooler climates and are replaced each season. They can be used to fill gaps in the border and to create beds of colour. However, they are most at home planted near the house or in containers, as strong-coloured annuals are often difficult to mix with the more subtle tones of permanent planting. Popular bedding plants, such as petunias, busy Lizzies (*Impatiens*) and marigolds (*Tagetes*), are available in a wide range of colours and varieties. Single colours provide the greatest impact, and the

Nicotiana sylvestris

gardener has more control over the effect of the planting. Designer-mixes of blended colours offer a softer alternative, and can be easier to mix with other plants.

Taller, more informal annuals, such as pinks (*Dianthus*), tobacco plants (*Nicotiana*, see also page 152) and cleomes (see page 152), are better mixed with herbaceous perennials and shrubs in the border than the smaller, more highly cultivated bedding plants. The tall, elegant ***Nicotiana sylvestris*** and the scented biennial ***Dianthus barbatus*** (sweet William) are ideal.

Most bedding plants like sun, but some succeed in shade (see page 135)

Dianthus barbatus

Gaultheria procumbens • *Primula vulgaris* • *Skimmia japonica* 'Rubella' • *Thymus* 'Doone Valley' • *Viola* •

Tulipa 'Pink Frosting' and *Narcissus* 'Salome' rise above the emerging leaves of hostas and a cloud of blue forget-me-nots (*Myosotis*).

SPRING- AND SUMMER-FLOWERING BULBS

Bulbs are reliable performers that deliver a wonderful show of colour for little investment. Some can be regarded as permanent residents in the garden, while others are best replaced on an annual basis. Most gardeners plant them with the thought that they will be there forever, or will move from pots into the open ground the following season. In reality, many are discarded after the first year, or are forgotten about and more are purchased the following season.

Daffodils (*Narcissi*) are popular for their reliable spring performance. They will appear and flower for many years, and are well suited to a wide range of soil conditions. Choose shorter varieties for exposed sites and avoid double-flowering cultivars, as the stems often break under the weight of the flowers. The disadvantage is their foliage, which often takes until midsummer to die down. Dwarf varieties, such as ***Narcissus* 'February Gold'**🏆, ***Narcissus* 'Jetfire'**🏆 and ***Narcissus* 'Hawera'**🏆, have smaller, narrower leaves and a more graceful habit. They are all good for naturalizing in grass or in flower borders. Avoid mixed daffodils – they flower at different times and the colour mix can be unpleasant.

Tulips are elegant and sophisticated flowers and offer a wide variety of flower form and colour. On damp, heavy soils most last for a season only, while on lighter soils – their preferred habitat – they will often perform for several years. The tall Darwin and lily-flowering varieties are excellent to plant with herbaceous perennials, where their blooms will rise above the emerging foliage. Tulip foliage is unattractive as it dies down, but this occurs usually within a month after flowering.

Narcissus 'Jetfire'

PLANTING BULBS

Tulips, daffodils, crocuses, hyacinths, lilies and most other flower bulbs are best planted in groups. Position them a few centimetres apart, according to the size of the bulb. If planted too sparsely they will lack impact. Include several clumps of the same variety together in a border where possible, to intensify the effect. Most mixed varieties tend to flower at slightly different times, and if planted in small numbers they will lack impact.

BULBS FOR POTS *Crocus vernus* subsp. *albiflorus* 'Remembrance' • *Fritillaria meleagris* • *Muscari armeniacum* •

Alliums are always popular for their unique flower forms and soft colours that combine well with most others. Flowering after the majority of the spring-blooming bulbs, they are useful to prolong the season. ***Allium hollandicum*** and ***Allium hollandicum*** **'Purple Sensation'**♕ both have medium-sized flowers on tall stems. The flowers fade to develop into attractive seedheads that persist in the border until late autumn. ***Allium cristophii***♕ and ***Allium schubertii*** are pale silver-lilac in colour, with large, more explosive flowerheads on shorter stems. Both are superb plants to add near the front of a border with silver foliage subjects such as artemisias (see page 103).

Lilies are good value garden plants. There are many varieties that flower from early summer through to early autumn. Their elegant flowers are long-lasting and frequently highly fragrant. Plant them in small groups of three to seven bulbs at least 10cm (4in) apart. Lilies like well-drained, fertile soil with plenty of organic matter. ***Lilium regale***♕ is the classic white fragrant lily, with a burgundy-pink flush on the reverse of the petals; it is a must in any garden. ***Lilium speciosum*** **var.** ***rubrum*** has reflexed white, pink-flushed petals that are heavily spotted with carmine. It flowers in late summer.

Allium hollandicum 'Purple Sensation'

POTS IN THE BORDER

Bulbs such as tulips and daffodils (*Narcissi*) planted directly in a border can be a nuisance after flowering is over: their fading foliage is unsightly, and it is easy to forget their position when cultivating the ground during their dormant season. If they are grown in terracotta or dark ceramic pots, and are unobtrusively dropped into position during the flowering season, they can be removed immediately afterwards. The pots can, of course, then be filled with annual bedding plants for a splash of summer colour.

Lilium speciosum var. *rubrum* flowers in late summer alongside *Sedum spectabile*.

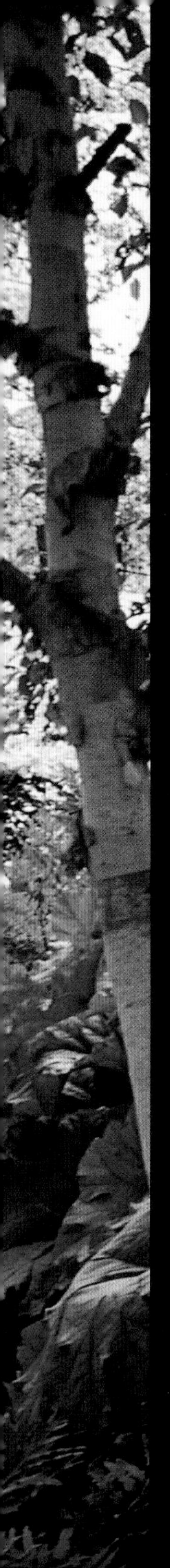

SITUATIONS

All gardens have unique characteristics that should affect their design, the choice of materials and the selection of plants. Certain conditions such as slopes, shade and lack of soil may affect just an area of a garden. In the case of a garden near the coast, a long narrow site, or the garden of a newly built house, the whole plot needs to be considered. None of these situations should be seen as disadvantages. If they are taken into account as part of the initial planning process, success can be achieved in just about any condition.

RIGHT: Moisture-loving perennials luxuriating in the dappled shade of birch trees at Savill Garden, Windsor.

Sloping sites

Slopes can be a challenge, both when you are establishing a garden and, later, when it comes to maintenance. Some gardens may have just one steeply sloped area; in other instances, the whole garden is on a slope. In either case, decisions will have to be made about levelling. The right choice of plant material is all important when planting on slopes.

Plentiful planting has softened this slope (above). Height in the foreground, contributed by *Catalpa bignonioides* 'Aurea', raises the planting at the bottom of the slope and emphasizes the colour theme.

There are various practical points to take into account before deciding whether to live with a sloping site or level it at the outset. The position and angle of the slope in relation to the house will have a major influence on design decisions. When a garden slopes towards the house, all of it is likely to be visible and open to scrutiny, so you need to give particular thought to what you want to conceal and how you will do this. You should also consider a drainage system, to prevent run-off (water running off the surface) damaging the property. A slope falling away from the house probably means the eye will fall

GOOD PERENNIALS FOR SLOPES *Aegopodium podagraria* 'Variegatum' • *Ajuga reptans* • *Alchemilla mollis* •

This is the same slope as the one shown opposite, before planting matures. The gradient has been divided with level areas of lawn. The steeper area of the slope (right) is retained using large pieces of rock to create planting pockets. The rocks are used in the gently sloping bed (left) to make a visual link between the various planted areas.

naturally on the view beyond the garden. By choosing trees and tall, eye-catching plants, you can bring the garden into closer contact with the house.

You also need to consider the aspect of the slope: a sunny, warm slope is a desirable environment for a wide range of plants, while a slope facing away from the main direction of the sun will be colder and therefore more challenging

TERRACING

Terracing is the creation of two or more level areas connected by either a short steep slope or a longer, more gentle slope. In a small, steep area, you will probably need some sort of retaining wall to support the level area (see page 114), and steps to link one level with the next. Where there is room for a more gentle slope between the level areas, a grassy bank is an alternative to steps, as long as the gradient is gradual enough for people to walk up and down it safely and easily. Steps take up less space, and can achieve a greater change of level, but they can be a problem for those who have difficulty climbing steps and when it comes to moving a wheelbarrow or lawn mower around the garden.

TO LEVEL OR NOT TO LEVEL?

A gently sloping garden is unlikely to cause major problems in design and construction. As long as levels are considered when constructing paved areas and lawns, the slope can be accommodated in planted areas. On a steeper slope, however, the practicalities of maintenance need to be taken into account in the design: mowing and movement of materials can be difficult and even dangerous if the gradient is very steep. If this is the case, levelling of an area or terracing of the site will probably be necessary. This is a decision you need to make at the outset: you will need special machinery or contractors to do the work. And bear in mind that terracing will change the soil profile.

Euphorbia cyparissias • *Geranium macrorrhizum* • *Lysimachia nummularia* • *Origanum vulgare* 'Aureum' •

Top: Timber sleepers have been used here to create broad steps on a gentle slope. The steps are easy to install and blend successfully with the planting. Above: Wire crates filled with terracotta pipes, tiles and pieces of stone make an effective and substantial retaining wall.

USING TIMBER TO CREATE RETAINING WALLS

On gentle slopes (1 in 10 or more), to support a change in level up to 50cm (20in) or so, the sleepers can be laid horizontally and anchored using metal pins driven through large drilled holes in the timber; steel reinforcing rods cut to length are ideal. A foundation of concrete 10–15cm (4–6in) thick should be laid under the sleepers. If this is made fairly wet, the timbers can be easily be levelled and settled into position.

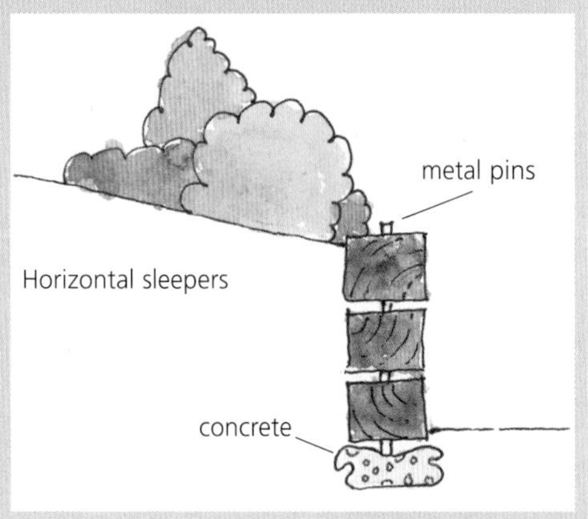

RETAINING WALLS

Retaining walls made from stone or brick are expensive to construct; they require substantial foundations and are best left to a professional. They can be made more cheaply using concrete blocks. To improve their appearance, you can render the blocks or cover them with self-clinging climbing plants, such as ivy (*Hedera*), *Ficus pumila* and *Euonymus fortunei*. Walls made in this way still need foundations. If the terraces are only going to take foot traffic and are not supporting any major constructions or buildings, retaining walls can be made from timber sleepers. In contemporary schemes, wire crates filled with stones, as used to retain roadway embankments, can look very effective, particularly when softened by planting.

PLANTING ON SLOPES

Planting on a steep slope is never easy. Choose a dry day and stand on hessian sacking to avoid slipping. Before planting, prepare the soil thoroughly by forking the individual planting stations and adding organic composted manure and slow-release fertilizer. When digging a planting hole, build up the soil on the downward side of the hole. This will help to channel rainfall run-off into the planting hole and will make any watering easier. Try to plant

GOOD PROSTRATE EVERGREENS FOR SLOPES *Cotoneaster dammeri* • *Cotoneaster salicifolius* 'Gnom' •

WEED-CONTROL MEMBRANE

Since maintenance is difficult on slopes, it makes good sense to use a weed-control membrane. This is a permeable covering that allows water to pass through to the soil but helps to prevent water loss and suppresses weed growth. First, rid the site of any perennial weeds, then lay the membrane over the soil surface. Pin it down with wire pins and bury the

edges to prevent it from blowing away. Make holes in the membrane, and plant the ground-cover shrubs through it. Always choose a black or brown membrane, which is less obtrusive than white or green.

Top: Broad, gentle steps set in grass transform a sloping lawn into an unusual and attractive feature.
Above: Raised beds built into a slope are easy to plant and to maintain.

in a slight depression for the same reason. Arrange plants in staggered rows rather than in straight lines. This will help to bind the soil and will be visually more pleasing. Water the plants in well, and water for several months after planting.

Short, steep slopes often exist on the boundaries of gardens where a central area has been levelled, or between level areas where a site has been terraced. They are often turfed or seeded because this is the cheapest option, although in the long run this causes a maintenance problem. Strimming such areas is hard work and inconvenient. Mowing is difficult and dangerous, even with the right sort of hover mower. Planting with ground-cover shrubs and perennials that will cover the ground and require little maintenance is the best solution.

Surface run-off can cause erosion of the topsoil. For this reason, it is vital to choose certain plants that will bind and hold the soil in position. Herbaceous perennials that form dense mats and low mounds are good choices. Also, shrubs

Gaultheria procumbens • *Hedera helix* 'Manda's Crested' • *Microbiota decussata* • *Pachysandra terminalis* •

Rosa rugosa
Ajuga reptans 'Atropurpurea'
Rubus tricolor
Rubus cockburnianus 'Goldenvale'
Ceanothus thyrsiflorus var. repens
Juniperus squamata 'Blue Carpet'
Vinca minor f. alba 'Gertrude Jekyll'
Lysimachia nummularia

with a suckering habit and those with dense, fibrous roots help to bind the soil. ***Rosa rugosa*** works well, and is particularly suitable for light, sandy soils disliked by most roses. It forms a mass of fairly upright, spiny stems with attractive apple-green foliage. The flowers are either single or double, in a range of colours from white, through shades of pink, to deep magenta. Large, tomato-like hips follow the flowers and persist on the plants, even after the leaves have fallen. ***Ajuga reptans*** **'Atropurpurea'** covers the ground with rosettes of bronze-purple leaves and spikes of sapphire-blue flowers in early spring.

The ornamental **brambles**, varieties of *Rubus*, are particularly good at colonizing ground. ***Rubus tricolor*** is a vigorous plant with trailing dark red stems and shiny green, heart-shaped leaves that turn bronze-red in winter. ***Rubus cockburnianus*** has arching, thorny stems up to 2m (6ft) high, covered with a white bloom that is revealed in winter when the leaves fall. ***Rubus cockburnianus*** **'Goldenvale'**♀ has bright gold, fern-like foliage and mounds of white stems in winter. It is a more compact plant, reaching 1m (40in) in height with a spread of 2m (6ft).

On sunny slopes, some of the evergreen **ceanothus** do an excellent job, covering the ground with mounds of glossy green foliage and binding the soil with their dense, fibrous roots. ***Ceanothus thyrsiflorus*** **var.** ***repens***♀ forms a broad mound up to 1 x 2m (3 x 6ft). The fluffy, mid-blue flowers are produced profusely in late spring and early summer.

Some **junipers** are found in the wild on limestone slopes with thin, poor soil. This makes them well adapted to growing in similar conditions in the garden. They are much more drought-resistant than many conifers. ***Juniperus sabina*** **'Tamariscifolia'** is low-growing and compact, with horizontal branches of bright green foliage forming a low,

GOOD PLANTS FOR ROCKY SITUATIONS *Baptisia australis • Dierama pulcherrimum • Kniphofia rooperi •*

flat-topped bush that makes dense, impenetrable ground cover. ***Juniperus communis* 'Repanda'**♕ is bronze-tinged in winter, with sprays of foliage that almost hug the ground. It does particularly well in full sun. ***Juniperus horizontalis*** (creeping juniper) hugs the ground as the name suggests. It has given rise to many cultivars noted for their blue-grey foliage. ***Juniperus squamata* 'Blue Carpet'**♕ is a low-growing conifer with spreading branches and dense, blue-grey foliage. It is good over rocks or low walls.

The periwinkle ***Vinca minor* f. *alba* 'Gertrude Jekyll'**♕ has fine stems and shiny evergreen leaves. The pure white flowers appear in spring. It is good in shade underplanted with snowdrops.

Lysimachia nummularia (creeping Jenny) has ground-hugging trailing stems and bright green leaves. The yellow flowers appear all along the stems in spring and early summer.

Mahonia aquifolium (Oregon grape) is useful on shady slopes. Its shiny, dark green foliage turns rich burgundy in autumn and winter, a perfect foil for the clusters of yellow flowers in early spring. It forms a low clump of stems up to 50cm (20in) high. There are a number of cultivars: ***Mahonia aquifolium* 'Apollo'** is particularly fine, with rich, glossy foliage and large clusters of flowers. (See page 81.) ***Mahonia aquifolium* 'Cosmo Crawl'** is shorter and more compact.

VARIETY OF HEIGHT

There is always a temptation to clothe a slope with prostrate plants. This accentuates the sloping appearance of the ground. Some variation in height will be more pleasing, and the slope can be used to increase the three-dimensional appearance of the garden. Taller plants, such as *Dierama dracomontanum* Wisley Princess Group (above), and a variety of different shapes, are as essential on a slope as they are on any level site.

ROCK GARDENS AND SCREES

Slopes offer the ideal conditions for a rock garden or scree-type planting. Scree is a natural habitat occurring in mountainous regions. During the weathering process, rock outcrops shatter into small, broken rocks and stones, and soil gradually develops deep below the surface. This creates a very well-drained growing environment, which is ideal for plants that need moisture at their roots but grow best through a layer of dry stones.

Sempervivums creatively planted in slate scree, among a herringbone of slate pieces set vertically into the ground.

For both rock gardens and scree beds, Mediterranean plants are ideal. Cistus, lavenders, brachyglottis, santolina and other silver-leaved plants all look good, particularly when combined with big pieces of limestone or slate. Alpine plants, such as saxifrages, and spreading dwarf conifers, for example ***Pinus mugo***, are also appropriate, and combine well with granite and sharp, grey grit. Other types of stone for rock gardens and scree-type plantings include water-washed cobbles, large pebbles and flints.

THINK BIG

When creating a rock garden or scree bed, it is vital to include large boulders, and to ensure there are plenty of them. A common pitfall is to use a small number of undersize rocks, which creates a 'currant bun' effect, with sloping soil dotted with pieces of stone. For a natural effect, lay rocks of different sizes in layers to simulate strata. Planting should also be large and bold –too many diminutive detail plants will be lost and out of scale.

Coastal gardens

Coastal gardens present a real challenge if you try to impose traditional country-garden principles on them. Lush lawns and flower-filled herbaceous borders will be difficult to achieve in maritime situations, as many plants struggle with the salt-laden air and free-draining soil. However, the lack of trees, the reflected light from sand, pebbles and stone, and big skies create a special environment for magical gardens that suit their surroundings.

Lavatera × clementii 'Rosea' thrives by the coast and blooms profusely from late spring to autumn.

Coastal gardens contain relatively little green, so the emphasis is on different shapes and textures. Flowers tend to be pure bright colours, and foliage is usually silver, grey and blue. The mesmerizing presence and movement of the sea is always there, even if not directly visible, so use its compelling influence in your design. Space, simplicity and minimal sophistication are the keys to success. Choose plants carefully, and try to use natural materials whenever possible.

PLANTS FOR SEASIDE GARDENS

Plants that tolerate coastal conditions have a delicate beauty – the soft colour and texture of their foliage belies their tough constitution. In their favour is the warming, maritime effect of the sea; frost is rarely a problem, so plants that may perish inland will grow here. The disadvantage of a coastal site is that winds – salt-laden for much of the year – have a desiccating effect in addition to the physical damage they cause.

Plants with silver foliage and those with sticky or aromatic leaves are usually suitable for coastal planting; the latter may contain oils to prevent them from drying out. Those from Mediterranean regions are also likely to be suitable.

Because of the subtlety of the surroundings and soft foliage, the seaside garden is the place for bright, loud colour – pure white, bright orange, vivid cerise, bright blue and shocking pink. Sun-loving plants recognize this and respond with an amplified display. **Calendulas, alyssum,**

A HINT FROM THE NAME

When choosing plants for a seaside garden, look out for plants with the following specific names, which indicate their maritime origins and will be suitable for a coastal site.

littoralis (e) – meaning 'of sea shores'

maritimus (*um*) (*a*) – meaning 'of the sea'

OTHER HEDGING AND SHELTER SHRUBS *Atriplex halimus* • *Cotoneaster simonsii* • *Euonymus japonicus* •

Agaves and other exotic plants grow well in the mild climate of coastal gardens. Here, the dramatic blue-grey leaves of *Agave americana* make a bold statement with the bright blue door and porch.

Lampranthus spectabilis

eschscholzias, **mesembryanthemums**, such as the magenta daisy ***Lampranthus spectabilis***, and other annuals grow vigorously and seed freely in gravel and stones. Many overwinter, providing an early display the following spring.

SHELTER AND HEDGING SHRUBS

Hedging shrubs and shelter shrubs can provide shelter from the wind in seaside gardens. While the former are usually trimmed, the latter are large and generally untrimmed and can provide more substantial shelter for larger gardens.

Elaeagnus* × *ebbingei is evergreen, with dark green leaves with silver undersides. It grows quickly to 3m (10ft) and its tall, upright branches are flexible and very wind-resistant. The small, creamy-white, fragrant flowers in autumn are an added bonus. It can be grown as a free-growing shelter shrub or planted 1m (40in) apart and trimmed as a tall, tough hedge. For a greener alternative, choose ***Griselinia littoralis***♀, from New Zealand. An upright shrub with round, olive-green leaves on yellow-green stems, its colour is highly unusual, resembling seaweed in coloration. There are variegated forms, but they are slower-growing.

The evergreen **escallonias** are splendid shrubs for seaside gardens, with their

Griselinia littoralis

glossy, sticky foliage and attractive white, pink or red flowers produced from late spring to early autumn. They are probably the best choice of hedging plant for a coastal situation, but the taller varieties, such as ***Escallonia* 'Donard Seedling'**♀

Pittosporum tenuifolium • *Pyracantha* SAPHYR ROUGE ('Cadrou') • *Quercus ilex* • *Rosa rugosa* • *Viburnum tinus* •

and **Escallonia 'C.F. Ball'**, can also be used as shelter shrubs.

Another useful shrub is ***Hippophae rhamnoides*** (sea buckthorn), which will cope with any amount of wind. Although not an evergreen, its thorny, angular branches act as an excellent wind filter in winter. In summer, its silver leaves are a lovely sight.

The **olearias**, again from Australia and New Zealand, are often difficult to place in inland gardens but are at home by the sea. ***Olearia macrodonta*** (New Zealand holly) grows to 3m (10ft) or more, with sage-green, holly-like evergreen leaves, which are silver on the underside. It is regarded as one of the best screening and shelter shrubs for coastal gardens.

Olearia macrodonta

ALTERNATIVE SHADE

In windy seaside gardens, trees are hard to establish and parasols can blow away or get damaged in the wind. A plain calico sail is a good, simple way of providing shade and can be left in position when the outdoor seating area is in use in the summer months. The sail can be inexpensively constructed by attaching it to a simple pergola structure, and can be removed and stored when not in use.

Eucalyptus pauciflora subsp. *niphophila*

Tamarix ramosissima

TREES FOR COASTAL GARDENS

Trees can be difficult to establish in a coastal garden, as their height exposes them to the ravages of the wind. Gardens right on the seafront and those on higher, exposed land behind the beach are the most challenging.

Some conifers, pines in particular, succeed. Where space permits, ***Pinus pinaster*** (maritime pine) is an excellent choice, with its long needles and reddish-brown bark. It makes a large tree in time, as does ***Pinus nigra*** (Austrian pine). For smaller gardens, ***Pinus mugo*** (mountain pine) is a possibility. Usually seen as a sprawling shrub, it makes an attractive small tree if it is grown as a single-stemmed specimen.

Most **eucalyptus** do well in a seaside garden; they are suitable in both habit and colour, and have the additional bonus of attractive bark that blends with stone. ***Eucalyptus pauciflora* subsp. *niphophila*** (snow gum) is one of the smallest, hardiest and most slow-growing eucalypts, with grey-green leaves and green and cream patterned bark.

Arbutus unedo (Killarney strawberry tree) has the advantage of wonderful cinnamon-coloured bark, white flowers and strawberry-like fruits. Although it is ericaceous, it tolerates lime and is very gale-tolerant. ***Arbutus unedo* 'Atlantic'** is a selected form that flowers and fruits freely, even as a young plant.

Tamarisks (*Tamarix*) are either large shrubs or small trees. At their best, they are a beautiful, light mass of graceful plumes of foliage and tiny, delicate flowers. At their worst, they are a twiggy mass of bony branches and sparse sage green. Hard-pruning of some stems after flowering is needed to maintain their vigour and performance. ***Tamarix ramosissima*** flowers in summer, and ***Tamarix tetrandra*** flowers in late spring and early summer.

For a more traditional deciduous tree, a **hawthorn** (*Crataegus*) is hard to beat. ***Crataegus persimilis* 'Prunifolia'** is a beautiful small, spreading tree, with rounded, glossy green leaves that colour rich yellow and orange in autumn. The white flowers in spring are followed by large red fruits that persist after the leaves have fallen. It grows to around 5m (15ft).

SHRUBS, PERENNIALS AND BIENNIALS

Silver foliage shrubs and perennials always succeed in coastal gardens. The sun-loving ***Lavandula angustifolia*, *Brachyglottis* 'Sunshine'**, ***Santolina chamaecyparissus*** and ***Helichrysum italicum*** are the basic essentials.

MORE TREES FOR COASTAL GARDENS *Acer pseudoplatanus* 'Atropurpureum' • *Ilex aquifolium* • *Laurus nobilis* •

Hydrangea macrophylla

(See page 103.) They provide soft, silver mounds of foliage that are easy to maintain in the airy atmosphere of a seaside garden. Trimming back after flowering in summer, and again in early spring, will keep them in good shape and covered in fresh silver shoots.

Rosmarinus officinalis (rosemary) and ***Salvia officinalis*** (sage), both evergreen shrubs, combine well with silver foliage perennials, providing not only foliage effect but also attractive blue flowers in spring and summer respectively. The poor soil and open aspect of a coastal garden result in oil-rich foliage, which is excellent for culinary use. (See page 83.)

Helianthemums and **cistus** both do well, providing they are sheltered from salt winds; choose the lower-growing varieties of cistus, such as ***Cistus* × *obtusifolius* 'Thrive'**.

Hebes thrive in coastal sites, free from the leaf-spot diseases that can be such a problem in humid inland gardens. The varieties of ***Hebe albicans***♀ and ***Hebe pinguifolia*** are particularly suitable to grow with other mound-forming sun-lovers. In sheltered sites, the large-leaved, more flamboyant hebes can be grown. These are often affected by frost inland, but by the coast their lush foliage is unscathed. ***Hebe speciosa*** cultivars have very showy bottlebrush flowerheads. ***Hebe* 'La Séduisante'** has bright crimson flowers and purple-tinged foliage.

Lavateras prefer the dry conditions of coastal gardens to the heavy, damp soil they are often subjected to in country gardens. The felted foliage and flexible stems are resistant to wind, and their delicate flowers are freely produced. ***Lavatera* × *clementii* 'Rosea'** ♀, with its bright, deep pink flowers, is unbeatable in this setting. (See page 118.)

The mophead and lacecap varieties of ***Hydrangea macrophylla*** thrive by the coast and provide a long-lasting display of blooms throughout summer and autumn.

The soft forms of many coastal plants need sharp contrast to bring them to life. The sword-shaped leaves of **phormiums**, **cordylines** and hardy **palms** have long been favoured in seaside gardens. Out of place in many situations, they are at home here, and their leathery leaves are well protected against the weather.

Alcea rosea (hollyhock) is a hardy biennial that seeds freely in sandy, well-drained soil. Its tall flower spikes of open bell-shaped flowers can reach well over

Hebe speciosa (1); *Alcea rosea* (2); *Santolina chamaecyparissus* with *Helianthemum* 'Ben Ledi' (3); *Cistus* × *obtusifolius* 'Thrive' (4); *Erigeron karvinskianus* (5); *Thymus vulgaris* with *Helichrysum italicum* (6).

Populus alba • *Prunus cerasifera* 'Nigra' • *Salix alba* var. *sericea* • *Sorbus aria* 'Majestica' • *Sorbus commixta* 'Embley' •

SUITABLE SURFACES

If you are planning to incorporate grass in a seaside garden, use a drought-resistant mixture. Lawns on sandy, coastal soil tend to be fine, tufted grasses rather than the more lush tufted and creeping grasses. These are adapted to dry conditions, and because of the well-drained soil they put on little growth, even during the summer months when other lawns need cutting regularly. It is difficult to achieve a lush, rich green sward in a coastal area, and in small spaces it is probably best to avoid a lawn altogether. An attractive alternative to a lawn would be gravel interspersed with low aromatic plants, such as varieties of ***Thymus serpyllum***.

If you are having paving, it should be in keeping with the pebbles and gravel used in the garden, and these, in turn, should relate to those from the beach if in close proximity. Light limestone or grey-green paviors are usually more appropriate in seaside gardens than yellow-buff shades. Natural bleached or colour-washed decking is at home in coastal sites more than in any other garden environment. Keep it simple, and never compromise on the quality of timber. Use thick boards that will cope with the rigours of rain and strong sunshine. Algal growth is rarely a problem in coastal areas, so decking is unlikely to become slippery in winter, unlike in an inland garden.

USING BOTTLES IN PAVING AND WALLS

Green and blue glass is very effective when incorporated in paving and walls, adding a little of the colour of sea and sky into the fabric of the garden. Empty bottles should be filled with dry sand before they are cemented carefully into place, leaving just the bottom of the bottle visible and level with the wall or paving surface. Providing the glass is firmly supported by the surrounding construction, it is quite safe used in this way for decorative purposes.

Top: A simple bench nestles in a sheltered corner of a flower-filled seaside garden. Centre: *Thymus* Coccineus Group forms fragrant mats in gravel. Above: Hardwood timber decking turns silver and bleached in bright sunshine and salt air.

2m (6ft) high. ***Erigeron karvinskianus*** colonizes dry, sunny situations lacking in soil. Its wiry stems carry a profusion of delicate daisy-like flowers from spring through to autumn. It is useful planted to soften walls and paving. (See page 121.)

ACCESSORIES AND FURNITURE

Coastal gardens lend themselves to accessories originating from the beach: ropes, driftwood, lobster pots, chains and all of the various pieces of flotsam and jetsam associated with boats and the shore. Items that would be quite out of place in most gardens sit comfortably here, and pieces of metal and wood that would usually be discarded can become important pieces of sculpture.

OTHER GOOD PERENNIALS FOR COASTAL GARDENS *Centranthus ruber* • *Crambe maritima* • *Erigeron* 'Dimity' •

Modern sculpture and contemporary accessories fit into the rather surreal setting of a simple gravel coastal garden; the simplicity of modern designs is complemented by the stones and textural forms of coastal plants. Large natural driftwood sculptures are dramatic and beautiful. A well-chosen piece may be expensive, but it may be the only structure needed in the garden apart from gravel, pebbles and plants.

Bleached wood or simple metal furniture works best in this setting. Teak left untreated is the obvious choice and will last for many years. Reclaimed teak is used to create some interesting, alternative furniture that can work well in this simple environment; the furniture then becomes a feature.

Simple, colourful deckchairs can be used to provide more comfortable seating in good weather. A scrubbed plank of wood supported by two plinths built from stone and pebbles may blend in as a permanent fixture better than a traditional bench would.

Fuchsia magellanica var. *molinae* blooms all summer with pelargoniums and the sapphire blooms of agapanthus. Left: Miscellaneous items collected from the beach are grouped to make a unique hanging wall feature.

REARRANGING THE PICTURE

In an informal seaside setting, objects found along the coast can become part of a garden sculpture collection. Since gardeners living near the shore are frequently beachcombers, new objects will often be added to the display. The items can be moved around regularly, together with pebbles, shells and gravel, to create an ever-changing picture and provide movable points of interest.

SEASONAL BEDDING PLANTS FOR SEASIDE GARDENS

When choosing seasonal bedding plants to add further colour, stay with the theme set by the permanent residents. Choose drought-resistant sun-lovers, such as pelargoniums and gazanias, in strong colours. These are ideal in pots and containers, and their tolerance of dry conditions cuts down on the need for regular watering. Hanging baskets are not a good choice for seaside gardens because of the windy conditions, which means they dry out quickly and get battered. Instead, choose glazed terracotta wall pots.

Eryngium maritimum • *Lathyrus grandiflorus* • *Lathyrus maritimus* • *Scabiosa* 'Butterfly Blue' • *Silene schafta* •

Corners and courtyards

Most gardens have areas where there is no soil to plant in, for example paving, concrete and steps. And some gardens, particularly small town courtyards, are made up entirely of hard surfaces, offering no opportunity to plant directly into the ground. In such situations, planting has to be approached differently, by using containers and raised beds.

An opulent planting scheme has been created here, using a variety of seasonal and permanent planting in an array of complementary and colourful containers.

If you are putting down a hard surface with the thought of using pots and containers, it is worth keeping some ground available alongside walls and fences in which to plant climbers, particularly adjacent to the walls of the house. Many climbers can be grown successfully in pots, but maintenance and watering is much easier if they are in the ground. It also enables you to position other containers in front of the climber to screen its lower stems – these are often the least attractive part of the plant.

Those faced with a bare concrete yard have several options. The hard surface will make an excellent foundation for paving. If this is the chosen option, then take drainage into account when the paving is being laid. If there are no planting beds for the water to run off into, it will have to be channelled into any existing drains.

Gravel or stone chippings are an inexpensive and simply installed solution. Gravel makes a good base for containers, and over a period of time the plants in the pots often root through into it. This has the advantage of additional anchorage, and means they can draw water from the gravel. Different sizes of

PLANTS FOR ARCHITECTURAL EFFECT IN POTS *Chamaerops humilis* 'Vulcano' • *Fatsia japonica* • *Laurus nobilis* •

GOLDEN RULES FOR CHOOSING CONTAINERS

• Choose the largest containers you can that are in proportion with the space. Small containers dry out quickly, blow over easily and look lost in large spaces.

• When choosing containers for permanent planting, it is vital to consider the shape. Pots that taper in at the top make it difficult or even impossible to extract the plant when repotting. Usually the result is damage to the plant and/or the container.

• Select colours and finishes that are sympathetic with the style of the garden and other materials used. Bright, colourful pots look out of place in traditional settings.

• Opt for simple designs. Plain pots are usually the best choice. The plant should be the most important addition to the pot, not the pattern on its side.

• Avoid inexpensive sets of pots. These look like good value, but usually the smaller sizes are of no use except to smash and use as drainage at the bottom of the larger sizes.

Juniperus communis 'Compressa'

Top: a group of simple pots of impatiens in the same colour makes a dramatic feature. Above: foliage plants such as hostas, here adding interest at the base of climbers on a courtyard wall, are ideal for permanent planting in pots.

stone and a variety of colours can be used to demarcate areas and create additional interest. Stepping stones can be set into the gravel to create a path and draw the eye to areas or points of interest.

A solid base, such as concrete, also makes an excellent foundation for wooden decking. This works well in a small space if combined with gravel around the edges to assist with drainage. A gravel border to house the majority of the containers keeps irrigation water off the decking and helps to prevent algal growth and resulting slippery conditions.

The combination of plant and container is crucial to its effect and impact as a garden feature. Top (left to right): *Tulipa* 'World's Favourite' in a fibreclay container; *Polystichum setiferum* 'Herrenhausen' in a stone urn; *Pleioblastus auricomus* in a glazed oriental pot. Above (left to right): *Chamaerops humilis* 'Vulcano' in a terracotta pot; trailing pelargoniums in a wooden barrel; carex in salt-glazed pots.

CONTAINER GARDENING

In many ways container gardening gives greater versatility than gardening in the open ground: plants in pots are easily moved, which means plants can be changed more easily and more frequently than in permanent plantings. Pots can be grouped and re-arranged, bringing those with current interest to the fore. And those gardening on chalk, for example, find they can grow acid-loving plants.

The size of plant material need not be greatly restricted: anything can be grown in a container, from the smallest alpine to a fairly sizeable tree. In principle, gardening in containers is no different from planting in the border. You have plants that provide permanent height and structure, and you add seasonal colour with bulbs and bedding plants (see pages 106–109).

The flexibility of gardening without any open ground is so appealing it may be that the owner of a small garden will make the decision to dispense with beds, borders and a lawn and put down a hard surface instead. Maintenance is easy, and there is the opportunity to take much of the garden with you if you move house.

SHRUBS FOR CONTAINERS AND RAISED BEDS IN SUN *Convolvulus cneorum* • *Hebe* 'Red Edge' •

RIGHT POT, RIGHT PLANT

Top: a group of glorious blue-grey glazed pots planted with a variety of shrubs and perennials. Front (left to right): *Astelia chathamica*, *Sambucus nigra* 'Eva' ('Black Lace'), *Melianthus major*, *Choisya* 'Aztec Pearl', *Helichrysum* 'Korma'. Back (left to right): *Chamaerops humilis* var. *argentea*, *Zantedeschia aethiopica*. Above: a simple, contemporary bowl filled with *Anemone blanda*.

The marriage of plant and container is an art form. If you get it right, you have more than a plant in a pot, you have a garden feature, a piece of living sculpture that will contribute more than any statue or manufactured ornament. It is worth buying the plant and pot at the same time if you are choosing something for a specific location.

The popularity of container gardening has resulted in a bewildering availability of different types of container. Choice will be largely dependent on the individual taste of the gardener. As with anything else in the garden, the colour and material of the container should be sympathetic with the property and the garden.

Stone containers are very traditional, and good quality ones convey an air of permanency. Bear in mind that their walls are thicker than those of terracotta or plastic pots, so choose a larger size to allow sufficient volume of compost for the plant's roots.

Terracotta and ceramic containers are the most popular, and are produced in enormous quantities in many regions of the world. Frost-resistance varies depending on the clay used and on the firing temperature; if this is a concern, check the level of frost-resistance with the supplier. These containers can offer exceptional value for money, and inexpensive ones are readily replaced. They are generally the best choice for most situations.

Traditional lead containers are lovely but expensive. They are a good investment for a classic, traditional location where they are to be a feature in themselves. Some of the new, fibre-clay imitations offer a real alternative to traditional lead. They are light, inexpensive and durable.

Plastic containers are inexpensive, light and unbreakable. They rarely look good in the garden and should be considered as

CONTAINER GARDENING TIPS

• Always raise the container slightly off the ground. This prevents the pot from becoming waterlogged by allowing free drainage, and also prevents earthworms from entering via the drainage hole. Although beneficial in the open ground, worms are harmful in the confined environment of a container.

• Always use specially formulated potting compost; garden soil will be a problem in the confines of a container. Loam-based compost always gives the best results, as its small particles have a greater capacity for retaining water and nutrients.

• Put a generous layer of stones or broken crocks in the bottom of the pot for drainage. In a large, broad container this should be about 6cm (3in) deep. In a small container, do not rob the soil depth to provide this much drainage.

• Allow space at the top of the pot for watering. The compost level should be a few centimetres below the top of the pot to allow you to flood the surface; this will also allow space to top up with fresh compost rather than repotting in the first few years.

• Use a controlled-release fertilizer once or twice a year. This is ideal for plants in containers, because it releases nutrients only when the soil is moist enough and the weather sufficiently warm for growth.

ALTERING THE PERSPECTIVE

Containers are an excellent way of adding height into the foreground, thereby increasing perspective. In a small space, this can make the garden look larger. In a large area, where planting can be lost in the distance, pots are a way of bringing the garden near the house.

utilitarian growing containers rather than elements of design. They are occasionally useful hidden behind other pots, or when placed inside porous containers to house subjects that resent drying out.

Resin, steel, zinc, bronze and other materials have been used to create various contemporary containers for all levels of budget. In a modern setting, they can look stunning when planted with simple architectural subjects such as grasses, yuccas, phormiums and palms.

Wooden containers are a good choice where a large vessel is needed. Oak half-barrels sit well in the traditional English garden and take rougher handling than ceramic containers of similar proportion. Wooden containers have good proportions for plant roots; broad and deep, they are ideal for larger subjects such as trees.

Reclaimed containers can be fun and quirky. Reclamation yards, local sales and second-hand shops produce a myriad of possibilities for creative planting – the only limit is your imagination. Old buckets, cans, dustbins, watering cans, baths and baskets are just a few possibilities that can be brought to life with the addition of a few plants.

RAISED BEDS

Permanent raised beds are another option. They provide a greater volume of soil than containers and more closely resemble the way plants grow in garden borders. By raising the plants above ground level, they are readily accessible – ideal for the less agile gardener.

Raised beds are easily constructed with brick, rendered blocks or wooden sleepers (see page 114). They need good drainage, so put a deep layer of hardcore in the base and, if the walls are of brick or rendered blocks, make drainage channels in them to prevent waterlogging. The deeper the bed, the larger the plants that can be grown; a 60–75cm (24–30in) depth of soil is sufficient for most plants.

SHRUBS FOR CONTAINERS AND RAISED BEDS IN SHADE *Buxus sempervirens* 'Elegantissima' •

A raised bed is ideal for groups of plants that require the same conditions: acid-loving plants, such as **rhododendrons**, **azaleas** and **camellias** for example.

Alpines and dwarf conifers also work well in raised beds. Add extra grit to the growing medium to improve drainage, and cover the surface of the compost with sharp grit. An alpine bed needs an open, sunny position.

In a shady corner, try a bed of **ferns**, **hostas**, **pulmonarias** and **ivies** (*Hedera*). Evergreen ferns and ivies will provide winter interest. Add pieces of wood, mossy stones and logs between the plants to complete the picture, and plant dwarf flowering bulbs – for example **daffodils** (*Narcissi*), **irises**, **crocuses** and **cyclamen** – for seasonal interest.

Compact evergreen shrubs are ideal in raised beds. When combined with perennials, bulbs and seasonal plants they provide all-year-round interest. (See pages 80–83 and 106–109).

As with pots and containers, raised beds should be filled with a good-quality growing medium containing loam. This will need feeding with a controlled-release fertilizer, and some of the compost will need replenishing annually.

A RAISED WATER GARDEN

A miniature water and bog garden can be created by lining a raised bed with plastic or butyl pondliner (see page 55); even a small, shallow pool amid the planting in the bed will attract wildlife. Primulas, astilbes and laevigata irises are choice, colourful perennials that will enjoy these conditions. Add *Cornus alba* 'Sibirica Variegata' or *Cornus sanguinea* 'Winter Beauty' for colourful stems that will provide interest in the winter, when most of the perennials die down.

GROWING VEGETABLES IN RAISED BEDS AND CONTAINERS

A raised bed is ideal for growing vegetables; even a small, shallow bed will produce a good crop of salad leaves, French beans, herbs, carrots or even potatoes. By choosing the more decorative vegetables, such as beetroot, lollo rosso lettuce and Swiss chard, a raised bed of vegetables can be an attractive feature: flowers such as marigolds and poppies can be added for colour. An open, sunny position is essential for growing vegetables.

Euonymus fortunei 'Emerald 'n' Gold' • *Euonymus fortunei* 'Silver Queen' • *Sarcococca confusa* •

Naturalized in grass, *Camassia leichtlinii* subsp. *leichtlinii* sparkles in the dappled shade of *Betula utulis* var. *jacquemontii*.

Shady areas under trees

A large mature tree contributes an air of maturity to a garden – it is very likely it was there before the garden was created, and in some cases before the house was built. The tree may well outlive this stage in the garden's history, so it should be respected and appreciated for the asset it is. Make use of the shade cast by trees by including attractive planting or perhaps a seating area beneath.

Although a blessing in many ways, a large mature tree can also pose problems to the gardener. It will undoubtedly cast shade over some of the plot, and its roots demand water and nutrients at the expense of those available to other plants. Deciduous trees shed their mantle each autumn, so leaves will have to be removed if there is a lawn, as they can cause problems if left on grass.

SURFACES UNDER TREES

If you are planning to have grass under a tree, it is vital to choose a seed mixture that has been specially formulated for dry, shady conditions. Normal mixtures will struggle or fail, resulting in thin growth and bare patches. Under trees with low canopies, it may be better to dispense with grass altogether and plant suitable ground-cover plants (see strip below) or cover the ground with gravel or bark chippings. A seat or appropriate ornament will complete the picture.

Decking is not a good choice under trees. It will quickly become covered in algae and will be slippery in winter. The same is true of smooth paving. Use a rougher, natural stone-effect slab set randomly; wide joints filled with gravel

GROUND-COVER PLANTS FOR SHADE *Asarum europaeum* • *Geranium macrorrhizum* • *Hedera colchica* •

SOFTENING PAVING

Paving can be softened with planting between the stones; this is effective in shade, and helps to join the hard surfaces to the softer parts of the garden. If the area is more to look at than walk on, *Soleirolia soleirolii*, mind-your-own-business (right), works well in this situation. It will need to be kept in check now and then. This is easily achieved by pulling the excess growth off the stones and treating the edges with a herbicide, taking care to keep the weedkiller away from other plants. In warmer climates buffalo grass (*Buchloe dactyloides*) can be used in a similar way, the strap-like leaves creating a shaggy fringe between the stones.

IMPROVING CONDITIONS

The range of plants that you are able to grow beneath a tree increases considerably if you carry out the procedures known as crown-raising and crown-thinning. These allow more sunlight to penetrate and improve air circulation. Consult a professional, qualified tree surgeon before embarking on this task.

Crown-raising involves removing some of the lower branches; this improves air circulation, and enables sunlight to find its way under the canopy, particularly when the sun is lower in the sky.

Crown-thinning involves removing some branches in the head of the tree. This allows more light to penetrate from above, resulting in dappled shade rather than heavy shade.

facilitate drainage. For ease of installation and maintenance, gravel is unbeatable. There is rarely any need to put down a membrane under trees, as most annual weeds struggle to germinate in the dry conditions. Small spring-flowering bulbs, such as **crocuses** and dwarf **narcissi**, can be planted in the gravel for early colour. Where conditions are not too dry, **heucheras**, ***Ophiopogon planiscapus* 'Nigrescens'**♀ and ***Liriope muscari***♀ add foliage interest at the edge of a gravel area in shade. (For further details on hard surfaces, see pages 48–51.)

PLANTING UNDER TREES

Choosing the right plants is the key to success in a garden under the shade of trees. Select plants that you know will stand a good chance of survival, rather than those that may possibly struggle and fail to deliver flowers because of the lower light conditions.

The plants that grow in a garden shaded by trees will lead the design of the garden if you let them, and in most cases this is the best approach. Bold evergreens will inevitably predominate, creating a wonderful feeling of calm seclusion in a garden. The dominant colour will be green, so for interest try to include a variety of shades, leaf shapes and plant forms, and use variegated foliage to lighten the picture.

TREE SEATS

A fitted tree seat around a large, mature tree offers a place to perch and enjoy the view. Its circular shape suggests that one could sit anywhere, so this kind of seat really only works well around a tree with an outlook in all directions.

In an interesting combination of foliage shapes and forms, evergreens, grasses and perennials with gold and variegated leaves lighten a bed that is shaded by trees.

Lamium maculatum • *Lamium orvala* • *Pachysandra terminalis* • *Rubus tricolor* • *Vinca major* • *Vinca minor* •

SHRUBS FOR DRY SHADE

Aucuba japonica (spotted laurel, see page 78) is made for shade. Growing to 2m (6ft) or more, it is an excellent structure shrub, providing bold, glossy evergreen foliage and attractive berries on some female cultivars. In very dry conditions, blackening of the new shoots can occur, but the plant quickly recovers. There are numerous cultivars: ***Aucuba japonica* 'Rozannie'**🏆, with broad, dark green leaves and plenty of red berries; ***Aucuba japonica* f. *longifolia* 'Salicifolia'** has narrow green leaves and red berries; ***Aucuba japonica* 'Marmorata'** is one of the best variegated forms, with dark green leaves, boldly splashed with gold.

Buxus sempervirens🏆 (common box) and its cultivars are useful as free-growing shrubs and to introduce trimmed and trained subjects into a shaded area. The variegated forms are particularly useful for their small, cream-edged leaves. ***Buxus sempervirens* 'Elegantissima'**🏆 is the best, with tiny leaves edged with creamy white. It is slow-growing so requires little maintenance. (See page 77.)

All evergreen **euonymus** thrive in shade on any soil. The cultivars of ***Euonymus fortunei*** are useful for their lax habit and attractive, bright foliage. (See page 81.) ***Euonymus fortunei* 'Emerald Gaiety'**🏆 is especially good at brightening a dark corner with its silvery-white-edged foliage. It will climb given the chance, so may be encouraged to embrace the base of a tree. (See Good Companions, opposite.)

PLANTING ON ACID SOILS

Gardens with tree cover on acid soil will find no shortage of plants to grow. An informal, naturalistic woodland design is the obvious choice. Rhododendrons, azaleas (above), camellias, leucothoes, gaultherias and pieris will all thrive, providing there is adequate moisture in the soil. There can be a problem when pines are the trees creating the shade, as their shallow, fibrous roots compete with the similar root systems of ericaceous plants; on sandy soil conditions, this may lead to stress and wilting of plants in the lower layer during the spring and summer. Do not attempt to plant too close to the trees, and choose the most open situations where rainfall can penetrate.

TRIMMED BOX IN A DESIGN FOR SHADE

Gravel studded with various sizes of trimmed box balls, perhaps combined with ceramic or stone spheres, could be a contemporary scheme for a small shaded garden. The box spheres would look good underplanted with a small-leaved ivy (*Hedera*) or periwinkle (*Vinca*).

HOW TO PLANT UNDER TREES

Autumn is the best time to plant under deciduous trees, as the plants then have the whole winter to establish themselves before the leaf canopy thickens and reduces the amount of rainfall reaching the plants. Water is at a premium in such situations because of competition with the trees.

When planting under trees, it is particularly important to prepare the ground thoroughly. Dig out the planting holes using a sharp spade that will cut through any tree roots you come across, and incorporate plenty of planting compost, ideally one that contains a water-retaining compound, which will help the roots to get going. Use a controlled-release fertilizer at the planting stage, and reapply the feed once a year, at the start of the growing season. Keep the plants really well watered during their first season until they establish themselves in the surrounding soil. Do not plant too close to a mature tree: anything substantial needs to be planted at least 3m (10ft) away if it is to thrive.

OTHER GOOD SHRUBS FOR SHADE *Camellia japonica* • *Camellia* × *williamsii* • *Daphne pontica* •

***Euonymus fortunei* 'Silver Queen'** is the loveliest of all the *fortunei* cultivars: slow-growing, its cream-edged foliage and sprawling habit are ideal for the smaller garden. (See page 99.) For a more substantial shrub, ***Euonymus japonicus* 'Chollipo'**♕ is unbeatable, with its erect growth and rounded dark green leaves edged with creamy yellow. (See Good Companions, below and page 101.)

× *Fatshedera lizei*♕ is a sprawling shrub with large, glossy green palmate leaves. It is a tolerant creature that is useful with variegated ivies (*Hedera*) and euonymus. The white-variegated **× *Fatshedera lizei* 'Variegata'**♕ works well in front of dark green aucubas and laurels (*Prunus lusitanica* and *Prunus laurocerasus,* see page 77). The most striking cultivar is **× *Fatshedera lizei* 'Annemieke'**♕, with leaves with a central blotch of lime green. (See Good Companions, page 135.)

Ilex × altaclerensis 'Golden King'

Viburnum tinus 'Eve Price'

The **hollies** (*Ilex*) all grow well in shade, as they originate from woodland habitats. The variegated forms of ***Ilex* × *altaclerensis*** and ***Ilex aquifolium***♕ are bright, cheerful plants, with striking foliage that will brighten the darkest corner. Once established, they grow well under trees but are slow to grow in their early years. ***Ilex* × *altaclerensis* 'Golden King'**♕, with its dark green leaves broadly edged with rich gold, is one of the best hollies. A female variety, it will berry well, holding its fruit well into the New Year if birds leave them alone. The golden-variegated ***Euonymus fortunei* 'Emerald 'n' Gold'**♕ makes a good planting partner if other plain evergreen shrubs such as ***Sarcococca confusa*** and the laurel ***Prunus lusitanica*** are present in the mix. (See page 81.) For creamy-white variegation, ***Ilex aquifolium* 'Ferox Argentea'**♕ is a good choice. (See Good Companions, left.)

Mahonias are tough evergreen shrubs with holly-like foliage that succeed in shade on any well-drained soil. ***Mahonia japonica***♕ has pale yellow flowers in winter and early spring (see page 85). The brighter yellow ***Mahonia* × *media* 'Charity'** is vigorous and upright, and flowers in autumn and winter. ***Mahonia* × *media* 'Winter Sun'**♕ is more compact, with upright sprays of yellow flowers. See also ***Mahonia aquifolium* 'Apollo'**♕, pages 81, 117.

With its holly-like foliage, ***Osmanthus heterophyllus* 'Variegatus'**♕ makes a mounded bush up to 1.2m (4ft) high. The leaves are bright with white edges and are smaller than those of holly. (See Good Companions, page 135.)

Viburnum tinus grows just about anywhere, and is one of the few shrubs that will grow successfully under oak trees. Its dark foliage, pink buds and white flowers are a familiar sight in

GOOD COMPANIONS

Euonymus japonicus 'Chollipo'♕ (1), with its creamy-yellow-edged leaves, is striking when planted with a camellia of similar flower colour, such as *Camellia × williamsii* 'Jury's Yellow'♕ (2).

The creamy-white holly *Ilex aquifolium* 'Ferox Argentea'♕ (3) mixes comfortably in shade with *Viburnum tinus* or the bright red winter stems of *Cornus alba* 'Sibirica'♕ (4).

The porcelain flowers of *Viburnum tinus* 'French White'♕ (5) make an excellent companion for *Euonymus fortunei* 'Emerald Gaiety'♕ (6) *and Osmanthus heterophyllus* 'Variegatus'♕.

Elaeagnus pungens 'Maculata' • *Fatsia japonica* • *Prunus lusitanica* 'Variegata' • *Symphoricarpos × chenaultii* 'Hancock' •

FABULOUS FOLIAGE FOR SHADE

With a leafy canopy above, a structural backdrop of bold evergreens, and a green carpet filling the space between paving and gravel, dappled shade is the perfect setting for fabulous foliage plants. The lower light conditions improve the definition of leaves. While in strong sunlight, they become reflective and their intricate beauty may be lost in the middle of the day when the sun is overhead; in shade their beauty is always apparent.

Hostas and pulmonarias work well in shade, provided there is adequate moisture. The larger-leaved hostas, such as *Hosta sieboldiana* var. *elegans*♀ (1) and *Hosta* 'Frances Williams'♀, are dramatic from the moment their bold shoots push through the ground in early spring. Their ribbed and corrugated leaves are sculptural and dramatic, and both make superb subjects for pots. (See also pages 94–95.)

Some of the **pulmonarias** (2) have foliage to rival any hosta, with silvery spots and markings that last throughout the season. They are a good choice in gardens where slugs and snails are a problem. Good varieties include *Pulmonaria saccharata* 'Leopard', *Pulmonaria longifolia* 'Ankum' and *Pulmonaria* 'Roy Davidson'.

Ferns are perfect in the woodland atmosphere created by overhanging trees. Evergreen ferns are useful for their winter interest, while deciduous ferns delight with their fresh green unfurling fronds in spring. Exotic tree ferns can be dramatic features in this setting. A group of three ***Dicksonia antarctica*** ♀ tree ferns of varying heights will make a statement bold enough to build a planting design around. When underplanted with other lower-growing ferns, such as ***Polystichum setiferum* 'Pulcherrimum 'Bevis'**♀ (3), the tree ferns become part of the garden rather than standing like awkward visitors.

gardens. In smaller spaces, choose the compact ***Viburnum tinus*** **'Eve Price'**♀. (See page 133.) Where a larger plant is required, the free-flowering ***Viburnum tinus*** **'French White'**♀ is excellent. (See Good Companions page 133.) ***Viburnum tinus*** **'Variegatum'**♀ does not have the most robust constitution but does well in shade. In sun and in exposed situations, its creamy-variegated leaves tend to brown around the edges. (See Good Companions, opposite.)

Tiarella cordifolia

GROUND-COVER PLANTS

A host of horizontally growing herbaceous perennials and climbers succeed under trees, and create an interesting and varied carpet that can be used as a setting for features and underplanted with bulbs. **Ivies** (*Hedera*), **periwinkle** (*Vinca*) and **euonymus** are obvious choices. The large-leaved ivies are often ignored in favour of the smaller, more delicate-leaved varieties; however, they work well and create a lush, opulent carpet. ***Hedera colchica*** **'Sulphur Heart'**♀, with its large, gold-brushed, glossy green leaves is stunning under the dark green leaves and red stems of *Prunus lusitanica*.

Another good evergreen is ***Euphorbia amygdaloides*** **var. *robbiae***♀, which has underground creeping stems, giving rise to upright stems up to 60cm (2ft), with dense whorls of shiny evergreen foliage and lime-green flowers in spring. (See Good Companions, opposite.)

Tiarella cordifolia♀ is an evergreen perennial with heart-shaped leaves and fine stems of light green flowers. Not the showiest of perennials, it provides delicate relief when planted with large-leaved ivies and bergenias.

OTHER GOOD FERNS FOR SHADE *Adiantum venustum* • *Asplenium scolopendrium* • *Asplenium trichomanes* •

ADDING COLOUR

Bulbs are the obvious way of adding colour in a shaded garden. Those that hail from woodland habitats are natural choices, as they are adapted to the environment. Most provide early colour before the leaf canopy thickens and robs them of light and water.

Narcissi, *Hyacinthoides non-scripta* and ***Muscari armeniacum*♀** all grow successfully amongst herbaceous ground cover under trees. **Crocuses, *Anemone blanda*♀, *Eranthis hyemalis*♀, *Scilla siberica*♀** and ***Puschkinia scilloides* var. *libanotica*** need gentler planting companions that will not smother their fragile blooms; they work particularly well when planted in gravel. Some bulbs flower in autumn – ***Cyclamen hederifolium*♀** and ***Colchicum autumnale*** for example, which provide a surprising splash of summery colour under the leaf canopy.

Hyacinthoides non-scripta

Most bedding plants need sun to grow and bloom successfully. However, there are some that tolerate shade. They rarely do well when planted in the ground under trees, as conditions are just too dry during their peak growing season. Grow them in pots or containers in the sunniest part of the garden and move them into position once established. Use special container compost with a water-retaining agent

Impatiens walleriana 'Accent Cranberry'

for optimum results. The best summer bedding plants for shade are **busy Lizzies** (*Impatiens*). Available in a wide range of colours, they are versatile, long-flowering and reliable. **Begonias** also grow and flower well without sun. The small-flowered ***Begonia semperflorens*** varieties are reliable although their colours tend to be rather hard. The dark foliage varieties lose leaf colour in shade. **Fuchsias** flower well in shade and many will survive the winter in open ground.

GOOD COMPANIONS

Osmanthus heterophyllus 'Variegatus'♀ (1) works well with blue spring-flowering bulbs, such as *Muscari armeniacum*♀ (2), and with white-variegated hostas and silver-spotted pulmonarias.

Try growing the creamy-variegated *Viburnum tinus* 'Variegatum' (3) with the light green, creamy-margined leaves of the ivy *Hedera colchica* 'Dentata Variegata'♀ (4) as ground cover.

The lime green in the leaves of × *Fatshedera lizei* 'Annemieke'♀ (5) is accentuated when planted with the lime-green flowers of *Euphorbia amygdaloides* var. *robbiae*♀ (6) or *Alchemilla mollis*♀.

Cyrtomium fortunei • *Dryopteris affinis* • *Dryopteris erythrosora* • *Dryopteris filix-mas* • *Polypodium vulgare* •

Big spaces

Those with small gardens may look enviously upon gardeners with large plots and lots of space to accommodate all the plants they desire, but owners of large gardens are likely to reciprocate the feeling when maintenance tasks become arduous and difficult to keep up with. In addition to the extra maintenance, one of the main challenges of a large plot is to create a garden that is interesting and personalized, as well as in keeping with the surroundings, particularly if it is in a country location.

When designing a garden for a large plot, the gardener needs to decide at the outset whether to divide the area or use the big space as a whole. Smaller areas focus the attention of the visitor more than one large space, but a divided plot will be harder work in terms of detail and maintenance: each garden within the garden will have its own requirements.

Using the plot as a whole will need vision on a grand scale, and placing key plants and features requires some thought. You will need to consider how trees relate to one another and how they look from the house as well as from various positions in the garden. Anything that draws the eye, such as a gazebo or summerhouse, will look different from different angles; those angles are inevitably wider and the distances greater in a large space. A photo survey helps when designing the garden, and enables you to draw on to the photographs the changes you are planning to make (see page 35). On the ground, canes and posts in key positions give an idea of how things will look. Leave them in position for a few days and live with them before making any final decisions.

Finer detail should be reserved for smaller parts of the space, where it will be noticed. During the early years of garden design, small, manageable areas were enclosed near the house for the purpose of ornamental gardening – this is a useful principle to observe.

The view from the garden: planting around the house provides a link with the garden landscape.

BASIC PRACTICALITIES

In most cases, large gardens are not for perfectionists. Those who like their edges trimmed, not a blade of grass out of place and not a weed in sight will find a big garden frustrating. Although acceptable from a distance, most large plots reveal their imperfections on closer inspection. The only solution to perfection in a big space is to employ help: the larger the space, the more you will need.

Large gardens need adequate storage facilities for all the gardening equipment, tools and machinery required, a fact that needs to be considered at the planning

In this large garden the planting is more detailed around the sitting area adjacent to the house. This is the most frequently used and most visible part of the garden.

Trees and shrubs encroach into a large, open space, providing interest and softening the boundaries.

stage. Ideally, the storage area should be close to where the equipment will be used, or you may need to consider a trailer; moving tools, compost and garden waste around a large garden is laborious as well as time-consuming.

GARDEN FEATURES

One of the hardest things to achieve in a large garden is the incentive to encourage the visitor to explore. When planning the space, try to include a focal point, such as a garden feature, pavilion or other structure at the end of a large, open space, to invite the visitor to venture out into the further reaches of the plot (see pages 56–63).

A hard-surfaced area will usually be needed near the house as a sitting area. If the garden is one big, undivided space, the patio needs to be sufficiently large to be in proportion. Substantial, heavier furniture is usually the best choice for a large garden; a small, light, four-seat patio set will look lost if it is the main set of furniture. Other seats and furniture may well be appropriate elsewhere in the garden, but this comes later.

In a big garden, large stone flags or paving slabs look better than small paviors. Appropriate planting around the paved area will increase its apparent size, and will help to blend the hard surface into the soft element of the landscape. The planting should be relatively wide and bold, and can be low to preserve the view; a narrow border with diminutive plants will look lost.

GARDEN WASTE

It is worth bearing in mind that large gardens generate a huge volume of garden waste. Adequate composting facilities are essential, as you won't want to take weekly trips to the recycling centre, and the garden will benefit enormously from the organic compost produced.

Unmown grass under trees creates a softly moving picture that changes with the seasons and the breeze. The grass is best cut in late summer before the leaves fall.

LARGE AREAS OF GRASS

Big gardens will, undoubtedly, have a large area of grass. If the plot is divided, the practicalities of moving mowing machinery from one area to another need to be considered at the outset. Probably a ride-on mower or tractor will be used. Paths between beds need to be wide enough for access, or you will end up using a push-mower as well.

Large, manicured lawns are hard work and, if created from scratch, they need careful preparation. They also need considerable upkeep. Even if you are going to do the mowing yourself, it is worth considering using a contractor for maintenance, feeding and management of moss and weeds.

Vast areas of grass are more interesting if the space is divided. Have your better-quality lawn near the house, extending from the main seating area, and rougher grass that is easier to maintain in other areas of the garden. Management of grass is easier if you are not too fussy about weeds. Clover maintains good, emerald-green leaf colour throughout the year, and should be welcomed in pasture-quality grass. A rougher grass mixture will be more resistant to wear and will cope with drought conditions more happily than finer grasses. In hot, dry weather, a large area is difficult or impossible to irrigate, so concentrate on a smaller area near the house and leave the rest. Remember, grass is better if not mown too short. If it is left a little longer before cutting, it maintains its fresh green colour for longer and does not enter the brown, dormant state as quickly in periods of drought.

WILDFLOWER AREAS

Large areas of grass can be cultivated as a wildflower meadow. This is not a low-maintenance option as many would imagine. As a rule, the poorer the soil, the better the wildflower population. To reduce soil fertility, it is important to remove the grass cuttings after mowing, otherwise they break down in the soil and increase its nitrogen content.

In a garden situation, meadow grass can be cut early in the season. From mid-spring it is allowed to grow and flower along with the meadow flowers. It is then cut as hay in midsummer. Ideally, it is left on the surface to dry for the wildflower seeds to fall through to the ground; then all mowings are removed and it is cut short for the rest of summer and autumn.

NATURALIZED BULBS

If you are planning to plant spring-flowering bulbs that will naturalize in grass, it is a good idea to plant them in large drifts close to trees. The grass can be left to grow around them while the leaves die down after flowering.

CREATIVE MOWING

Paths cut through long grass are interesting and inviting, and allow the development of different colours in the landscape as the grasses mature and reach their flowering stage. As the grass gets longer it has more movement, and the scene changes as the grasses catch the light at different times of day. The picture can be changed annually by mowing the paths in different positions.

Some wildflowers, such as poppies, need disturbed soil. In a meadow planting, pockets need to be resown every season. They quickly merge with the grasses and other flowers as the meadow grows.

On poor, well-drained soils, neglected pasture can be transformed into flowery meadow in a season or two. On moist, clay soils the effect is harder to achieve.

If you plan to create a wildflower meadow, consult a specialist seed merchant who deals in native flora. Not only is it important to get the right mix of fine meadow grasses, it is vital that it contains the right mix of indigenous flora for your area and soil type.

CHOOSING PLANTS

Whatever the setting of a large plot, when it comes to choosing plants think big. Trees and large shrubs will come into their own in a large space. Perennials can be planted in groups and drifts, and detail planting should be kept near the

In big spaces perennials can be planted in drifts. Here, a rich planting of *Aquilegia vulgaris*, *Meconopsis cambrica*, *Digitalis purpurea* f. *albiflora* and *Allium* 'Globemaster' creates a wonderful naturalistic effect.

PLANTS FOR BIG COUNTRY GARDENS

Some compact trees and obvious garden cultivars do not sit comfortably in a country setting. Instead, choose trees that fit into a rural environment, such as birch (*Betula*), beech (*Fagus*) and mountain ash or rowan (*Sorbus aucuparia*). The flowering dogwood, *Cornus* 'Porlock' (above) has a loose, natural habit and is a delight in early summer, when cream, pink-tinged bracts adorn the graceful branches. Here, they associate well with the white and grey bark of *Betula pendula* and the purple-pink blooms of the foxglove *Digitalis purpurea*.

house. Height in the foreground is still an important part of the scene, as it helps to frame the view and pull the boundaries into the picture. Avoid the tendency to try and fill a large space by planting lots of small, spaced-out individual plants – these just end up looking lost. Instead, keep the space open, but encroach into it with bold groups of trees and shrubs.

British native shrubs, such as *Euonymus europaeus, Viburnum opulus* and *Cornus mas*, work well planted in groups in grass. On acid soil, deciduous azaleas and hardy hybrid evergreen rhododendrons can be used in the same way in the dappled shade of trees.

TREE MAGNOLIAS

Those with large, sheltered gardens on neutral to acid, fertile soil should not deny themselves the indulgence of planting a tree magnolia. *Magnolia campbellii* (Himalayan pink tulip tree) is one of the most ravishing sights in flower and worth the wait from planting to first flowers. *Magnolia campbellii* subsp. *mollicomata* is a hardier form, flowering after only 10–15 years. The huge pink, waxy blooms are carried elegantly on the branches in mid-spring. The late Sir Harold Hillier wrote: 'I for one get great pleasure from planting a young *Magnolia campbellii*, for although I will never see it bloom, already I can smell its latent fragrance and see its flowers against a blue spring sky.'

GOOD TREES FOR LARGE GARDENS

One of the great delights of having a large garden is being able to grow larger trees to their potential. If starting from scratch, then choose some trees for the future and some that will reach maturity more quickly – that way you get the best of both worlds. Evergreen trees provide structure and colour throughout the year, while deciduous trees create a wonderful picture that changes with the seasons. In a large space you are able to appreciate all their attributes – shape, colour and silhouette – with leaves and without.

TREES THAT MATURE QUICKLY

Acer saccharinum (silver maple) (1) – A large, graceful tree with delicately cut leaves, which are silver on the reverse and dance in the wind. The branches sweep downwards as they mature. Has yellow, apricot and flame autumn colours.

Betula utilis var. *jacquemontii* (Himalayan birch) (2) – A large, broadly conical tree with white bark and a superb winter silhouette. The leaves are large for a birch, turn yellow in autumn, and provide good movement and shade.

Eucalyptus dalrympleana♕ (mountain gum) (3) – A fast-growing, hardy eucalyptus with beautiful white patchwork bark. The grey-green leaves are held elegantly on the branches. It is good when grown as a multi-stemmed specimen and planted in a group.

Liquidambar styraciflua (sweet gum) (4) – A must for gardens on neutral to acid soil. Although not the fastest grower, it makes an impact from an early age. It is often mistaken for a maple (*Acer*), and its shiny palmate leaves turn spectacular shades of red and burgundy in autumn, lasting well on the branches. *Liquidambar styraciflua* 'Lane Roberts'♕ is renowned for particularly fine colour. *Liquidambar styraciflua* 'Worplesdon'♕ is usually smaller, with more deeply cut foliage turning orange and yellow in autumn.

Salix alba subsp. *vitellina* 'Britzensis'♕ (scarlet willow) (5) – A large, fast-growing willow with upward-sweeping stems and delicate leaves; ideal on a damp site. In winter, the bare stems are orange-red.

TREES FOR THE FUTURE

Cedrus deodara♕(6) – A large, graceful cedar with branches drooping at the ends. It is a superb specimen tree to plant for the next generation.

Fagus sylvatica 'Riversii'♕ (purple beech) (7) – Nothing surpasses the majesty of a mature purple beech with its grey bark, downward-swept branches and magnificent deep wine-purple foliage. The young foliage is pale copper and a delight in spring; the old leaves turn brown and stay on the branches well into winter.

Juglans regia♕ (common walnut) (8) – Makes a stately tree with aromatic leaves and a graceful, broad frame. Mature specimens bear nuts; if you grow it for the fruit, plant a named clone, such as *Juglans regia* 'Buccaneer', as it will crop at an earlier age than others.

Liriodendron tulipifera♕ (tulip tree) (9) – A wonderful tree with tulip-shaped leaves that turn golden yellow in autumn. Curious green and gold flowers are produced on mature specimens. This tree is attractive when young, magnificent when mature.

Quercus palustris♕ (pin oak) (10) – A graceful oak with slender, drooping branches and sharply lobed oak leaves of shining green. It grows more quickly than many oaks and is attractive from an early age. The autumn colour is spectacular: rich scarlet and flame, and long-lasting.

Narrow spaces

Many gardens are long and narrow – only the width of the house and twice or more the length. Terraced properties often have these narrow spaces to contend with, flanked on either side by walls or high fences. Often these narrow spaces are accessible only through the house or – if you are fortunate – through a gate at the end of the garden.

A large terracotta pot planted with *Astelia chathamica* creates a bold focal point in a narrow space.

DIVIDE THE AREA

In a long, narrow garden, straight borders and paths running along its length to the end boundary accentuate the corridor effect, and should be avoided at all costs. The space can be made to look broader and in better proportion if it is 'divided' into different areas. You could use screens, arches and other physical barriers that allow access from one 'room' to another. A narrow space divided in this way creates an intimate effect, but some may find it claustrophobic. Alternatively, you can divide the space more subtly by changing the surface and character of the areas on the ground. For instance, you could include sections of paving, gravel, lawn, different planting areas or a water garden, with paths leading from one area to the next. This method still divides up the space while preserving the open nature of the garden. In small gardens, this may well be best option, as there are fewer structures taking up ground space.

PROVIDING PRIVACY

Narrow gardens and spaces alongside houses are often overlooked by neighbouring properties. In the quest for

HARD SURFACES

When creating a patio area in a narrow garden, design the area to be no longer than the width. Small paviors usually work better than large stone slabs in a narrow space. Random patterns of paving stones are often more successful than uniform rows, as the eye does not follow the joints down the garden, although tiles with smaller inserts can look stunning in a narrow town garden. For a more informal effect, keep the edge of the paving irregular to allow the planting to run into the paved areas. If using decking, you can create an illusion of width by laying the boards across the garden rather than down its length.

PLANTS FOR TRELLIS AND SCREENS *Abutilon* 'Kentish Belle' • *Actinidia pilosula* • *Jasminum officinale* f. *affine* •

This narrow garden has been cleverly divided to create an impression of width. A larger plant in a pot at the end of the garden would make a bolder focal point and take attention away from the door and gate beyond.

A narrow space can be divided into rooms, each with a different character. Left: seating areas on either side make the most of the sun at different times of day. Right: the journey through the garden is longer when the divisions run diagonally; this layout often makes the best use of the aspects of the garden. In both plans planting ensures the garden does not reveal all features at first glance.

privacy, the temptation is to plant tall hedges. However, these encroach on the garden and only make it appear narrower. Light timber or wire screens clothed in climbing plants are considerably more effective and take up less space. (See also pages 30–31.)

Rather than choose the highest solid fence available, opt for a lower panel with a trellis top, or a screening panel. These are less confining and allow more air and light into the garden. As boundaries are very prominent in a narrow garden, a more attractive option is well worth the investment.

Light colours increase the feeling of space, so this is worth considering if painting or varnishing boundary walls or fences. If in doubt, play safe and opt for the least obtrusive light colour and let the planting do the work.

CHOOSING PLANTS

Narrow gardens are often shaded for part of the day by boundary walls or fences, or by the house itself. The width does not allow for the cultivation of large, broad structure shrubs, and if screening plants are used for extra privacy, these may take up a large amount of valuable space.

In many gardens a narrow space exists at the side of the house, separating a property from its neighbour. This tends

CLIMBERS FOR NARROW SPACES

Climbers that stay close to their support are the ones to choose for the side boundaries in a narrow garden.

Akebia quinata (1) is a vigorous semi-evergreen climber. The pretty, pale green leaves, which are composed of several leaflets, are carried on twining stems and quickly make a light, attractive drape over a wall or trellis. The fragrant, red-purple hanging flowers appear in profusion in spring. It is a real bonus to have such an exotic climber early in the year.

Clematis like their roots in the shade and their tops in the sun. Therefore they will probably provide colour and interest at the top of boundary walls and fences but may display bare stems lower down. *Clematis* 'Hagley Hybrid' (2) is a reliable variety, growing to around 2m (6ft). The habit is fairly upright and the plant carries pink flowers with chocolate-brown stamens throughout summer. This is one of the best large-flowered clematis for a shady situation. The winter-blooming *Clematis cirrhosa* var. *balearica* is also a delightful, delicate climber, with dark green, fern-like foliage and soft, creamy-yellow, bell-shaped fragrant flowers.

Ivies are unbeatable for shady walls and fences. *Hedera helix* 'Oro di Bogliasco' ('Goldheart') (3) is a neat grower, with dark green leaves boldly splashed gold in the centre. Its straight stems work well when planted with *Jasminum nudiflorum*♀ (winter jasmine). Although the bright yellow flowers of the jasmine are a delight in winter, its stems are untidy and can be unattractive. By growing it with the ivy, the stems are concealed but the flowers are still visible.

The summer-flowering jasmines, although not the tidiest of climbers, are worth growing for their fragrant flowers and light, trailing growth. In warmer areas, the lovely *Jasminum polyanthum*♀ is unbeatable, with its dark green, fern-like leaves and richly fragrant flowers in late spring or early summer. Elsewhere, *Jasminum officinale* f. *affine* will grow prolifically and bloom through summer into autumn. Although not as free-flowering, *Jasminum* FIONA SUNRISE ('Frojas') (4) provides a longer season of interest with its golden foliage. In shade, this is a pleasing lime green, probably easier on the eye than the bright gold of the leaves in full sun. *Jasminum officinale* 'Clotted Cream' (5) offers a cream-flowering alternative, a pleasing change from the usual porcelain white.

Trachelospermum jasminoides♀ (6) is a wonderful evergreen climber with small, dark green leathery leaves and fragrant, creamy-white, jasmine-like flowers in summer. It likes the shelter of a narrow garden and, although it prefers some sun it does well in shade. The variegated *Trachelospermum jasminoides* 'Variegatum'♀ is attractive but slow to get going.

MORE CLEMATIS FOR NARROW SPACES *Clematis* 'Bill MacKenzie' • *Clematis* 'Broughton Star' •

HIDDEN SEATING

Seating arbours arranged opposite one another either side of a central feature, perhaps a self-contained water feature, create an interesting and intimate garden area. The seating will not be immediately apparent when looking down the garden from the house, and is unlikely to be overlooked by the neighbours. This is a good alternative to patio furniture in a small, narrow garden.

PLANTING TIPS FOR NARROW GARDENS

- The use of vertical space increases the garden area, so climbers, wall shrubs, light trees and tall, slim plants, such as fastigiate shrubs and conifers and the more compact bamboos, all help to make small, narrow gardens appear larger.
- Think small and compact, but also consider plants that are going to offer interesting structure and form.
- In a small area all plants must earn their keep and provide interest for much of the year. Avoid large, woody shrubs with a short season of interest, and perennials that take up space for just a few days of glory.
- When planning the garden, allow the open areas – the lawn, gravel or paving – to run the full width of the space at some point rather than planting heavily along the full length of the boundaries, which can make the area seem narrower.

to be a bit of a wasteland, owing to the difficulty of knowing what to grow there and how to use the space. As it is often overlooked by windows, it is well worth trying to make this area attractive with appropriate planting.

WALL SHRUBS

Many shrubs can be trained onto walls and fences, and these are often a more controllable choice than true climbers. All of the wall shrubs described below are tolerant plants that survive in the windy and draughty conditions that often prevail down the side of a house.

Flowering quinces have small, glossy green leaves and reddish new growth. The flowers appear in late winter and are a delight on the bare branches, before the leaves appear. Fragrant, yellow, quince-like fruits hang on the branches of some varieties in autumn. Colours range from white through subtle peaches and pinks to fiery scarlet. ***Chaenomeles* × *superba* 'Crimson and Gold'**♀ is deep red with golden yellow anthers.

Chaenomeles × superba 'Crimson and Gold'

Cotoneaster horizontalis is an easy shrub that grows on any soil. Its

Cotoneaster horizontalis

IVY SCREENS

Screens of ivy (*Hedera*) grown on wire mesh are used extensively in Europe, where gardens tend to be small. They can be made any height up to 2.5m (8ft), and are easily constructed using a heavy-gauge wire mesh supported on treated timber posts. Large-leaved ivies, such as *Hedera hibernica*♀, work best; plant two plants per metre run of mesh. The ivies will be slow to start with, but will quickly gain momentum and can be trained to fill the screen. Trim occasionally to remove some of the trailing shoots. Add small-leaved variegated ivies such as *Hedera helix* 'Glacier'♀ at the base, or an occasional large-leaved ivy such as *Hedera canariensis* 'Gloire de Marengo'♀ (right) for a lighter effect.

Clematis florida var. *sieboldiana* • *Clematis* 'Frances Rivis' • *Clematis* 'Fuji-musume' • *Clematis* 'Polish Spirit' •

herringbone branches carry small dark green leaves that turn rich red before they fall in autumn. Sealing-wax berries persist on the branches after the leaves have fallen. Growing to 2 x 3m (6 x 10ft), it is useful for low walls.

Several **euonymus** of trailing habit make good evergreen climbers and can be trained to keep them close to the wall. Both the white-variegated ***Euonymus fortunei*** **'Emerald Gaiety'**♀ (see page 79) and the golden-variegated ***Euonymus fortunei*** **'Emerald 'n' Gold'**♀ (see page 81) will climb if they are given a support.

Pyracanthas are easy to grow. They are evergreen, have fragrant white flowers in spring, and berries in autumn that last into winter. Although spiny, they are easily trained and controlled and will make an effective screen when grown on wires or a wire mesh.

Pittosporum tenuifolium 'Silver Queen'

NARROW EVERGREENS

Many evergreen shrubs can be pruned to assume a narrow shape. Plants used for trimming and training, such a **bay** (see pages 76–77) and **box** (see pages 76–77, 80), are obvious choices. ***Pittosporum tenuifolium***♀ varieties mostly grow into broad cones and respond to light trimming in mid-spring. ***Pittosporum tenuifolium*** **'Silver Queen'**♀ is a small-leaved cultivar with a dense habit, and is slower-growing than some varieties.

Pyrus calleryana 'Chanticleer'

Some fastigiate forms are unusual and attractive. ***Ligustrum japonicum*** **'Rotundifolium'** is a very slow-growing, compact form of the Japanese privet with round, glossy, dark green leathery leaves forming a sculptural column. ***Ilex crenata*** **'Sky Pencil'** is an extremely narrow, upright form of the Japanese holly, with small, oval, dark green leaves and rigid stems.

On a larger scale, ***Ilex aquifolium*** **'Pyramidalis'**♀ is a narrowly columnar holly when young, though it broadens with age. It has emerald-green foliage, is less spiny than many hollies, and is free-fruiting, with bright red berries in winter. ***Ilex aquifolium*** **'Green Pillar'** is spinier and more upright, and is also free-fruiting.

NARROW TREES

Interest above eye level is particularly important in a small or narrow space. The garden may already be shady, but that does not remove the need for trees. Trees may also increase privacy by screening the view from overlooking windows.

Many ***Prunus*** have a narrow, upright habit. ***Prunus*** **'Amanogawa'**♀, probably the best known, is lovely when in blossom, with its large, pale pink double flowers, but it lacks interest for the rest of the year and there are others that have more to offer. ***Prunus sargentii*** **'Rancho'** is an upright

KEEPING TREES TRIM

Some trees lend themselves to trimming to preserve a narrow shape. *Carpinus betulus* 'Fastigiata'♀ (see page 72) has naturally upright branches. If lightly trimmed when it reaches the desired size, it will maintain a narrow shape.

Sorbus aria 'Lutescens'♀ (below), with its silver-green foliage and compact head, can be kept as a compact tree if pruned in late winter, before the new foliage emerges. This tree is increasingly grown as a silver foliage column, with branches to ground level.

The variegated varieties of *Acer negundo* offer a bright alternative to plain foliage trees. They benefit from hard-pruning each spring, so can easily be maintained as small, narrow subjects. *Acer negundo* 'Flamingo' (below) is effective grown in this way, as pruning will encourage salmon-pink new growth.

MORE TALL, NARROW TREES *Acer campestre* 'William Caldwell' • *Fagus sylvatica* 'Dawyck Purple' •

MIRRORS AND METAL SHEETS

If the garden has a wall on one or both sides, mirrors can look good in a narrow garden. Opposite mirrors, perhaps in conjunction with *trompe l'oeil* trellis, can make a garden appear larger and are particularly effective when surrounded with greenery. Mirrors in gardens can be a hazard to birds that fly into them in error, although this is unlikely if the mirrors are on the side walls. Polished metal sheets can be substituted for glass mirrors. These are obviously safer and a softer reflection can be more effective.

The reflective surface of water and a mirror create an illusion of space in this small formal garden at the Chelsea Flower Show.

WATER IN THE GARDEN

Incorporating water in the garden always helps to create an illusion of space. (See pages 52–55.) The reflective surface of still water adds depth and therefore a vertical element. The sound of running water adds another dimension: even the smallest water feature will add atmosphere. The sound is amplified in a narrow space bounded by walls.

form of one of the most ornamental cherries. It is reasonably fast-growing, has mahogany-coloured shiny bark, flame and orange autumn foliage colour, and clouds of bright pink flowers in spring. ***Prunus* 'Spire'**♡ is an elegant, narrow tree with upright branches festooned with soft pink flowers in spring. The foliage colours red and purple in autumn. Widely grown as a street tree, it is an excellent plant for a tight corner.

The ornamental pear ***Pyrus calleryana* 'Chanticleer'**♡ takes some beating in a narrow space: it has a narrow conical head, white flowers in spring, followed by dense, pale green foliage that turns butter yellow in autumn. The leaves persist on the tree well into winter, before falling to reveal an elegant branch framework.

NARROW CONIFERS

Some conifers are especially useful in narrow spaces. Those with a narrowly columnar or fastigiate habit are excellent structure plants, providing an evergreen feature that can be used effectively to rise out of lower planting. They suit both traditional and contemporary settings.

The fastigiate forms of **yew** are particularly fine plants. The dark green Irish yew, ***Taxus baccata* 'Fastigiata'**♡, is superb as a slender youth, as a tall, dark and handsome adult, and as a slightly broader old man. It is an excellent plant to create an exclamation mark in planting, rising out of evergreen ground cover such as ivies (*Hedera*) or periwinkle (*Vinca*), and as a focal point planted at the end of a bed or path. The golden Irish yew, ***Taxus baccata* 'Fastigiata Aureomarginata'**♡, has the same dark, narrow leaves but with golden margins. These offer a lovely, lighter effect and look good with gold-variegated plants and against dark green, broad-leaved evergreens.

Taxus baccata 'Fastigiata Aureomarginata'

***Juniperus communis* 'Hibernica'**♡ (Irish juniper) makes a dense column to 3m (10ft) or more. Its prickly foliage is soft sage green and possesses the wonderful juniper fragrance. It is good in a formal design.

With the advent of milder winters, ***Cupressus sempervirens*** is a more common feature of northern European gardens than it used to be. Its narrowly columnar habit always seems to convey an atmosphere of the Mediterranean, and it is ideal with silver-leaved plants in sunny, drier gardens. Plants often produce plentiful heavy cones that tend to separate the foliage. Careful pruning will help to preserve a tighter habit.

Malus tschonoskii • *Quercus robur* f. *fastigiata* • *Sorbus aucuparia* 'Fastigiata' • *Ulmus* × *hollandica* 'Dampieri Aurea' •

New build: new garden

A new garden belonging to a newly built house is a real challenge. It is a wonderful opportunity because it is a blank canvas without the restrictions of existing features, but it is also a daunting prospect because the whole layout is down to you! Patience is vital: make sure you plan carefully, and prepare the ground thoroughly – tempting as it is to rush ahead, you will be much happier with the results in the long term if you take your time now.

The addition of heavy trellis to the top of a boundary fence brings additional privacy without a feeling of enclosure to this seating area. Climbing plants will quickly transform the structure and add maturity.

Although you will have invested heavily in a new house and perhaps feel you will never have any money to spend again, before you start work on the garden it is worth considering whether you will one day extend the property. Might you add a conservatory or a garage? Or extend the house itself? An extension changes the orientation of the house and garden, and may well occupy space you are about to spend money on surfacing or planting.

If you think there is a chance you may build an extension of any kind, take this into account when designing the garden.

Also consider the cost of materials. For example, if you are considering building a conservatory where a patio is planned temporarily, opt for gravel as a short-term solution rather than expensive paving.

It will not be a pleasing prospect for the new homeowner, but the first thing to do in the new garden is to tackle any building work. You will probably want a decent paved area, and you may want

IMPROVE THE SOIL

It is always worth carrying out a soil test to check the pH of soil in a garden, particularly in the case of a new build. The topsoil may well have been imported, so it may not be the same as soil in surrounding gardens. In most cases, you will need to incorporate plenty of organic matter in the form of well-rotted stable or farmyard manure – the natural balance and ecosystem of the soil must be restored if this is to be a successful garden.

VENTURE INTO THE CENTRE

When designing a garden from scratch, our natural instinct is to play safe, and stay as close to the boundaries as possible – we often feel vulnerable if we venture into the middle of the space. This is why in most new gardens the borders end up as a narrow strip following the line of the fence, with a void of grass in the middle. A little bravery in advancing into the middle of the space with a tree, a bed, water or a group of shrubs will transform the space into a three-dimensional garden.

Circular paved areas, a curved path and rounded grass mounds transform this rectangular plot into a landscape that is interesting when viewed both from the house and within the garden. Large specimen acers and bamboos contribute instant height and maturity.

to erect fencing or additional buildings. If your budget prevents you from doing this straightaway, at least do all the foundation work at this stage.

PREPARATION AND CONSTRUCTION

During the construction of a house the land takes considerable punishment: topsoil may be removed and replaced with soil from elsewhere, the ground tends to be compacted by heavy machinery and building materials, and rubble and debris are buried in the soil. Cement, plaster and other materials may actually pollute the soil, particularly near the house. For this reason, there is much preparation work that must be carried out before you can get going on the planting.

There will undoubtedly be rubble left in the garden, so begin forking over what will be the planting areas and remove all those broken bricks, bits of tile and concrete fragments. These will be ideal as hardcore for the shed base or as a foundation for the patio – incorporating

A NEW LAWN

Most new gardens include grass – the most instant way of creating a green environment. Here are a few rules to follow when creating a new lawn:

- Always buy the best-quality turf or seed – a green sward is perhaps the most undervalued component of a garden, and a low-quality product will only lead to poor results.
- Choose cultivated turf or grass seed that is right for your soil type or situation. Grass seeds are blended for specific situations and uses, and it is important you choose the appropriate one for your garden.
- Ground preparation and laying turf are both heavy, demanding jobs and it is important to get them right. It may be worth enlisting professional help for this stage in the garden's construction, even if you intend to do the planting of the beds yourself.

A utilitarian fence is transformed with a fast-growing climber, *Humulus lupulus* 'Aureus' and a border of shrubs and perennials. The boundary becomes an integral part of the garden, and space is not lost to a hedge of functional screening shrubs.

them in the garden will save the cost of waste disposal. Do not use any fragments of soft building block for building foundations as these crumble in time.

SETTING BOUNDARIES

Many new gardens are part of a development of several properties, and there is often an urgent desire to reinforce boundaries. Fences and hedges are usually a top priority, and you will probably want them to be as inexpensive and quick to establish as possible. At this point it is easy to make a decision that you will regret later. For example, a row of fast-growing conifers may screen you from neighbouring houses quickly, but in the long term it will steal space from your plot and rob your soil of water and nutrients. Similarly, a solid panel fence will enclose the property instantly, but a fence with trellis planted with climbers may well be a more attractive solution in the longer term. Consider the alternatives carefully. (See pages 30–33.)

DRAINAGE

Compaction can cause many problems in new gardens, and you may need to install a drainage system. If the lawn is sodden during the winter, with moss and liverwort present, water is unable to drain away through the soil. An exploratory excavation will reveal a lot. By digging down, you will soon see whether the water is trapped in the top 20cm (8in) or so, prevented from draining by a compacted pan (a hard, impervious layer beneath the topsoil). If this is the case, deep digging is required, to break up the pan. Incorporate some sharp grit and well-rotted organic matter to open up the soil and improve its structure.

If exploration reveals a more major problem, it may be necessary to install drainage. This is not as big a task as it sounds if you do it at the outset. Usually a basic drain alongside the patio and around the lawn will do the trick. If you raise the level of the lawn and the planting areas, adding quality topsoil, the surface will be free-draining and run-off will be collected in the drainage channel.

Often the main cause of wet areas is the run-off from hard surfaces onto areas of compacted ground. On heavy, clay soils and poorly drained sites, a deep, narrow trench filled with a large grade of stone chippings alongside the paved area is a good idea. This trench should then lead to a soak-away: a large pit below the soil surface filled with stones and brick rubble that will collect excess water. In all cases, leave a gap between paving and the wall of the house and fill it with gravel.

PLANTING TREES

Trees and basic structure shrubs are the first plants to put in place; the rest of the planting will be built around them. Trees create the most impact, and in a new garden are particularly important in establishing privacy. Bear in mind that as trees grow they will cast shade on the garden, so position them carefully and don't plant too many, however empty the plot may look in the early stages.

Choose a tree that will deliver interest for as much of the year as possible and will look good from an early age. Pretty blossom trees are good for a week or so in spring, but what about the rest of the year? The following trees have something special to offer over several seasons.

Malus × *zumi* var. *calocarpa* 'Golden Hornet'♀ is a good choice for those who love apple blossom; it produces plenty of blossom, followed by round, golden yellow crab apples. (See also page 73.)

Malus × *zumi* var. *calocarpa* 'Golden Hornet'

Sorbus 'Joseph Rock'

Prunus cerasifera 'Nigra'

Malus transitoria♀ has pink buds that open to fragrant, pink, white-blushed flowers that garland the spreading branches in spring. Tiny yellow, cherry-like fruits follow in autumn, persisting after a display of golden autumn foliage. ***Malus bhutanica*** is similar but more upright and so better for a smaller space.

Prunus cerasifera **'Nigra'**♀ produces neat, dark purple leaves on dark stems. A round-headed tree, it forms a cloud of tiny pink flowers in early spring before the leaves unfurl. Its foliage makes a great impact all year, even at an early age.

Sorbus hupehensis♀ is a very compact tree, ideal for small gardens. The blue-green leaves turn red in autumn, while the pink berries turn to white and remain on the branches throughout winter after the leaves have fallen. Its relative, ***Sorbus*** **'Joseph Rock'**, is also an outstanding small tree, with white flowers in spring and clusters of amber berries in autumn. Pretty, fern-like leaves turn rich amber, flame, red and purple in autumn.

ADDING SHRUBS

The first shrubs you plant should contribute to the structure of the garden. Evergreens are the obvious choice, as they look good all year round; some also

INSTANT IMPACT

When making a new garden, it may be worth buying time by planting some mature specimens. Many shrubs and perennials are offered in large sizes, and make an immediate impact on the garden.

The best plants to buy as mature specimens are structure shrubs and evergreens. You are gaining a year or two, and they will quickly establish the framework of the garden around which you can build the rest of the planting. Aucubas, osmanthus, hollies (*Ilex*) and viburnums will all contribute more quickly if planted in a more mature state. Architectural subjects such as palms and phormiums also need maturity to fulfil the role they are planted for, so a mature specimen plant will always be the best option. It is not worth buying short-lived and quick-maturing subjects as specimens.

FILLING SPACE IN NEW PLANTING

When you plant new beds with shrubs and perennials they will at first look very sparse: the impression will be too much soil and not enough plants. Annuals and flowerbulbs are invaluable for filling gaps until permanent subjects are established. Tall informal subjects such as *Cleome spinosa* (1) and *Nicotiana affinis* (2) are ideal for this purpose, and lilies such as *Lilium* 'Casa Blanca'♀ (3) are easy, inexpensive and provide exotic, scented blooms in summer.

1

2

3

FAST-GROWING SHRUBS *Buddleja* 'Lochinch' • *Cornus alba* 'Elegantissima' • *Hebe* 'Midsummer Beauty' •

have additional qualities, such as flowers or interesting leaf colour. Evergreen favourites, such as ***Choisya ternata*** (see page 38), ***Mahonia japonica*** (see page 85) and ***Photinia* × *fraseri*** **'Red Robin'** (see page 78), are shrubs you cannot go wrong with. They grow on any soil in sun or semi-shade, and you can control their size by pruning.

MAKING A NEW GARDEN YOUR OWN

Choosing the same plants and materials as your neighbours is a common pitfall in a new garden situation; after all, neighbouring gardens are a source of inspiration – and are often more visible in new developments. By choosing a few accessories you can make your garden individual, just as you will do in the house.

Garden structures, such as gazebos and arbours, add instant height to a garden and are easily personalized by colouring the timber and by the choice of furniture. Their greatest advantage in a new garden is the way they give you something to build the planting around. (See pages 56–59.)

Water brings a garden to life and adds sound, movement and reflection. (See pages 52–55.) If you are planning a pond, make it sooner rather than later. Digging out a pond, even a small one, generates a lot of excavated soil. Make your pond at the outset, and you can probably lose the soil elsewhere in the garden rather than having to remove it from the site.

Garden ornaments and pots personalize your plot (see pages 60–63). If you invest in a few items that you like, they can be with you for many years and can become part of other gardens that you may create: if you move, take them with you.

Top: An attractive arbour can be the centrepiece of a new area of planting. Centre: Water brings any garden to life. Right: A contemporary black marble statue makes a bold focal point. Far right: Slate strips set into planting draw the eye.

Lavatera × *clementi* 'Rosea' • *Phlomis fruticosa* • *Physocarpus opulifolius* 'Diablo' • *Pyracantha* 'Orange Glow' •

Index

Page numbers with suffix 'b' indicate plants listed across bottom of page. Suffix 'i' refers to illustrations.

INDEX

PICTURE CREDITS

The publishers would like to acknowledge with thanks all those whose gardens are pictured in this book.

All photographs were taken by John Hillier and Andrew McIndoe with the exception of:

Philippa Bensley: 96a, 144(3)
Sue Gordon: 126b
Kevin Hobbs: 68a, 75c
Jane Sterndale-Bennett: 97(3), 134a
Raymond Turner: 125c, 128a
Chris Twilley: 29c, 49c, 123a, 145c
Robin Whitecross: 38a

Artworks by Robin Whitecross: 54b, 67e, 114c, 143b, 143c